POKER
FACE

THE RISE AND RISE OF LADY GAGA

Poker

HYPERION

NEW YORK

Photo Credits

Frontmatter: *pp. i and xiii (half-title pages):* © Mario Anzuoni/Reuters/Corbis; *pp. ii-iii (title spread):* Brian J. Ritchie/Hotsauce/Rex/Rex USA. **Chapter openers:** © The Toronto Star/ZUMA Press. **Photo insert I:** *p. 1:* Seth Poppel/Yearbook Library; *p. 2:* Seth Poppel/Yearbook Library *(all)*; *p. 3:* Scott McLane / Retna Ltd. *(left)*, Josie Miner *(right)*; *p. 4:* David Ciemny *(top and bottom)*; *p. 5:* Jason Squires/WireImage; *p. 6:* Hal Horowitz/ www.halhorowitz.com *(top)*, © Chris Walter / Retna Ltd. *(middle)*, Yui Mok/PA Archive/ Press Association Images *(bottom)*; *p. 7:* © Planet Photos/ZUMApress.com *(left)*, Aaron Fallon/JBG Photo *(top right)*, Phil Poynter/Art-Dept.com/trunkarchive.com *(bottom right)*; *p. 8:* © Francois Berthier/Corbis *(top)*, © Mario Anzuoni/Reuters/Corbis *(bottom)*. **Photo insert II:** *p. 1:* Michael Buckner/Getty Images; *p. 2:* Scott Weiner/Retna Ltd.; *p. 3:* © The Toronto Star/ZUMA Press *(top)*; Theo Wargo/Getty Images for VEVO *(bottom)*; *p. 4:* Michael Caulfield/WireImage *(top left)*, Sonia Moskowitz/Globe Photos *(top right)*, WENN *(bottom and background)*; *p. 5:* Yui Mok/PA Wire/Press Association Images *(left)*, Splash News *(right)*; *p. 6:* Kevin Mazur/WireImage *(top)*, Brian J. Ritchie/Hot- sauce/Rex/Rex USA *(middle)*, Jeremy Kost/WireImage *(bottom)*; *p. 7:* Kevin Mazur/ WireImage *(top left)*, Brian J. Ritchie/Hotsauce/Rex/Rex USA *(top right)*, Larry Busacca/ Getty Images *(bottom)*; *p. 8:* Rennio Maifredi/trunkarchive.com, 2009.

Copyright © 2010 Maureen Callahan

Library of Congress Cataloging-in-Publication Data

Callahan, Maureen.
    Poker face / Maureen Callahan.
       p. cm.
    ISBN 978-1-4013-2409-4
  1. Lady Gaga.   2. Singers—United States—
Biography. I. Title.
    ML420.L185C35 2010
    782.42164092—dc22
    [B]
         2010020104

Hyperion books are available for special promotions and premiums. For details contact the HarperCollins Special Markets Department in the New York office at 212-207-7528, fax 212-207-7222, or email spsales@harpercollins.com.

Designed by Janet M. Evans

FIRST EDITION

10 9 8 7 6 5 4 3 2 1

TO BILLY

CONTENTS

ACKNOWLEDGMENTS

Deepest thanks and appreciation to Elisabeth Dyssegaard, who I was lucky enough to have as my editor, and Theresa Karle, Nina R. Shield, and all at Hyperion; to the peerless David Kuhn, and to Jessi Cimafonte and Billy Kingsland at Kuhn Projects; to Col Allan and *The New York Post* for its support, and editors Margi Conklin, Serena French, critic Elisabeth Vincentelli, and especially Steve Lynch for his generosity and insight.

This book would not have been possible without William Van Meter, Steve Knopper, Hal Horowitz, Carrie Borzillo, Alisa Wolfson, Laura Schy, Chris Barth, and Erica Futterman. And equally without the love, advice, and support of William F. and Mary Callahan, Billy Callahan, Marc Spitz, Lizzy Goodman, James Iha, Lara Behnert, Tracey Pepper, Sarah Mullins, Mrs. Eileen Kennedy of Sacred Heart Academy, and the late Paul Good.

"Stop feeding me bullshit. Tell me the truth."

—Lady Gaga, 2009

"I hate the truth. I hate the truth so much I prefer a giant dose of bullshit any day over the truth."

—Lady Gaga, 2010

POKER
FACE

PROLOGUE

Everything is going wrong. This was supposed to be the big
night, the unveiling of her first arena tour as a headliner, and
props, costumes, and chunks of the entire stage set, which
cost $1.5 million, are missing, stuck in a town just thirty-seven
miles away. This stadium, the Manchester Evening News Arena
in England, holds 21,000 people and is the largest in the UK;
more people come in and out of here every year than any other
venue in the world. Her show is sold out, and even though she
hates the idea of canceling, she's so distraught over the chaos
and lack of preparedness that she asks if it's possible. She's not
just putting on a pop show; she's staging an elaborate five-act
rock opera with some twenty costume changes, pyrotechnics,
and a hydraulic lift that will elevate her about twenty feet above
the crowd. Among what's missing: an enormous stone fountain
that's supposed to spout blood, topped with an angel and ac-
companied by gorgeously decrepit backdrop images, like the
black-and-white footage that looks straight out of the 1902
Georges Méliès film *A Trip to the Moon.*

Lady Gaga, unknown just eighteen months ago and now, at
twenty-four, the biggest star in the world, is told no. Canceling
is not an option; it'll cost too much. She may be an exacting
artist, but she is also a shrewd businesswoman. She relents,

but insists on rehearsing up until the doors are about to open.

So here are the Gaga fans, ages four to fifty-five, lining up outside the Manchester Evening News Arena at six o'clock on this drizzly, chilly winter night, three hours before showtime, excitedly, politely snaking down and around the block. Nearly all the girls—who outnumber the boys by about three to one— are dressed like their heroine, in numbers and fervor not seen since little girls donned rubber bracelets and fishnet headbands in homage to Madonna circa 1984. They're tottering and trembling on five-inch spike heels, dressed in Day-Glo colors, and have foregone pants in favor of long tops and tights; they've donned blond wigs and sunglasses and applied drag-queenish heavy makeup.

Also present are fifty-somethings on first dates; professors and other intellectuals; gay men in their twenties and thirties, many in Gaga-esque makeup; and prepubescent boys and girls with their parents, many in Gaga shirts. Dotting the entrance to the arena are the puzzled middle-aged men with makeshift stands hawking sub-par, unauthorized merch: If it has fur, or blinking lights, or better yet fur and blinking lights, they're selling it. They have no earthly idea what's going on—you can see it on their faces—but it's a recession, and scalped tickets for this show are starting at $150.

While a Lady Gaga performance circa 2009–2010 pulls from hundreds of postmodern pop-art threads, as derivative as it— as *she*—is, it remains wholly original. Gaga is smart enough to know that the limited number of songs in her very young catalog cannot sustain a two-hour set, but the spectacle she's created sure can. To Gaga and to her fans, "The Monster Ball," as she calls it, is not just a show: It is, as her life has become, interactive performance art of the highest caliber.

So the explosion of color and sex and kookiness and maybe some good old-fashioned pyro that a Gaga show promises is a huge deal in Manchester, as it will be two nights from now in Dublin. Manchester is a town under a permanently slate gray sky into which six-story slate gray granite buildings disappear. Not much happens except football; the town is home to two Premier League teams, Manchester United and Manchester City. Its lone four-star hotel, where visiting footballers stay, is a four-floor redbrick Marriott at the end of a cul-de-sac. Near that is a Grenada TV station, and it's a sliver of the size of the average American Costco.

That said, Manchester is known for producing some of the best bands in the world: Joy Division, Buzzcocks, the Smiths, the Stone Roses, Oasis. It's remarkable that swagger and solipsism, in equal measure, come from this painfully placid place. Like the Boston Red Sox or Canada, Manchester is perennially second best, forever dwarfed in size and status by London, yet always, somewhat poignantly, maintaining its competitiveness. It's been best described by Smiths lead singer Morrissey in the song "Everyday Is Like Sunday": "This is the coastal town/That they forgot to close down/Armageddon come Armageddon/Come Armageddon come."

Gaga's fans are happy to mill about the beer stands inside, taking a pass on opening act Semi Precious Weapons and waiting for her to take the stage. Her career may be in its infancy, but she's cultivated such loyalty from her fans that they will overlook, the way all who are newly in love do, imperfections big and small. They feel she does the very same for them. They hope.

"My worst nightmare," says a twenty-year-old college student named Gavin Dell, who is here with his best friend Carrie and who has used blue and gold glitter to create a fantastic lightning bolt over his right eye, "is that that's an image." Lady Gaga seems so sincere, he says, but it's also how sincere she seems that makes him fearful she's not. It's a generational thing, the irony of living in a post-postironic age.

"I would *hate* for that to be an image," he says. "Don't worry about me; I have a very busy life. But if this is all a press thing— that she's afraid of boys, of sex . . ." He's slightly, sweetly embarrassed by how invested he is in her, but he also can't help himself.

"It seems so genuine," he continues. "I hope to God it's true. Yes, she has stylists, but the perception is she's done it herself. *My* impression is she's done it herself. I might be wrong. But if I'm wrong, she's been very well put to me."

So: Just who is Lady Gaga, and how did she get to be that way? It's a question that's been asked of her over and over, from Ellen to Oprah to Barbara Walters, and she always gives the same answer: She was and is a freak, a misfit, a lost soul in search of her fellow travelers.

That line itself explains why this still very young woman— who grew up in comfort and privilege on New York's Upper West Side, whose musical heroes include Billy Joel, New Kids on the Block, and Britney Spears, who until two years ago considered

American Apparel avant-garde fashion—is so endlessly fascinating. Because to watch her open her European tour in Manchester is to search fruitlessly for the cracks between the girl who wanted to be the next Fiona Apple, a serious, sensitive singer-songwriter, and the glorious, demented art-freak performer on the stage.

When crowds in Europe are sick of waiting, they start doing the wave. And on this first night in Manchester, well on our way to half-past nine, they're doing the wave. Michael Jackson is playing on a loop, mainly everything off *Thriller,* and the message is none too subtle: This is the girl who has said she wants to be as big as Michael, a girl who, as he did, identifies herself as a freak show, whose own performances are, as his were, ghoulish in a childlike way, sexually provocative but never sensual, spectacles rife with pageantry but bolstered by state-of-the-art pop music delivered by an undeniably terrific, authentic voice.

There's a white scrim billowing in front of the stage, and just as the crowd is on the verge, the lights go down and the crowd erupts (all great rock acts do this—play with just how taut the rubber band can go before the audience is lost to them for good). A blue grid is projected onto the scrim, and a nebulous blob on the left begins to emerge and move toward the crowd, floating and swirling and taking shape as Gaga. A clock to the right of the screen rapidly runs down the seconds to start time; it hits 00:00:00:00, the scrim drops, and there she is, standing on the top of a staircase to the left, bracketed on one side by a fake storefront advertising, in neon lights, "Liquor," "Gold Teeth," and her own paradoxical brand, "Sexy Ugly." To the left is another industrial scaffolding, with the words "WHAT THE FUCK HAVE YOU DONE" spelled out in big white bulbs. She's opening with "Dance in the Dark," but the first minute of the song is inaudible over the din of the crowd.

Among the people and things Gaga will reference, overtly and covertly, on this night and in Dublin: *The Wizard of Oz;* the late designer Alexander McQueen's 2006 fashion show, in which Kate Moss appeared as a ghostly 3-D floating hologram; a famous image of McQueen binding a model—face painted white, streaks of red paint streaming from the eyes, mouth gagged with black ribbon—in swaths of white; the Broadway musical *Rent;* the archly art-directed interstitial clips MTV pioneered on its award shows; Elton John and Billy Joel; Rob Reiner's classic 1984 rock 'n' roll spoof, *This Is Spinal Tap;* the fashion-world satires *Brüno* and *Zoolander;* Cirque du Soleil; Japanese horror films of the 1950s; shock artists Tracey Emin and Damien Hirst; downtown New York provocateur Klaus Nomi and his London-based analogue Leigh Bowery, as well as New York City's later electroclash pioneers Fischerspooner; David Bowie and Freddie Mercury; Tina Turner in *Mad Max Beyond Thunderdome;* Sylvia Plath's poem "Death & Co."; Marilyn Manson; Walter Hill's 1979 cult film *The Warriors;* Grace Jones; Dale Bozzio of the eighties new-wave band Missing Persons; Irish dance phenom Róisín Murphy; the rave scene of the mid-to-late nineties and the entire gay culture, sub- and mainstream, of the past three decades; Sally Field in *The Flying Nun;* Fay Wray in *King Kong;* the stark black-and-white aesthetic of the great rock photographer Anton Corbijn; Wim Wenders's *Wings of Desire.* And, of course, Madonna.

The debt to Madonna is inarguably Gaga's biggest. Not only does she share a very similar origin story—good Italian-Catholic girl gone bad, working her way through downtown New York City's art and performance worlds with little money, possessed of a monomaniacal focus on becoming the biggest star in the world—but her career template and persona are also very much the same. Just as Madonna both stole from and helped mainstream gay culture through sexual provocation in her music, videos, and performances, her public playfulness with her own sexual orientation, and her early dedication to then-controversial causes like AIDS activism, Gaga, too, has done all of the above. Her live shows feature a lineup of shirtless male backup dancers, all shaved chests and oversized codpieces, that she calls "my gay boys." She's said that she's had sexual relationships with both men and women, though she also talks about wanting to find a nice man to marry and have babies with. She's an advocate for gay rights and, with Cyndi Lauper, part of M·A·C cosmetics' safe sex/HIV prevention campaign.

And, like Madonna, she is constantly shape-shifting, treating her persona like a malleable object, claiming each incarnation to be her authentic self, and now speaking, as Madonna once so maddeningly did, in a clipped, vaguely British accent.

But on these nights, in Manchester and conservative Dublin, in these arenas that have been transformed into the biggest, sweatiest, most wholesomely lewd dance parties on the planet, which will win raves in tomorrow's tabloids, Gaga's Madonna reference is very specific. (That Gaga regurgitates and reappropriates so many of her pop-culture precursors is, in itself, a meta-reference to Madonna.) The Madonna represented tonight, though, is the 1990 "Blond Ambition" incarnation, when she sported her Jean-Paul Gaultier cone-shaped bra, thick, level eyebrows, red lipstick, and yellow hair. But it's not Gaga who's dressed like that; it's one of the girls onstage.

In other words: Madonna is her backup dancer now.

ONE

CREATION MYTH

The first feat of Lady Gaga's young career: It was not that long ago that next to nothing of her personal life was known. There was no thread connecting her life three years ago to her life now as a super-high-concept, demographic-smashing global pop icon. This is deliberate; she doesn't study the lightweights.

The small details Gaga has doled out—she was a waitress, a working musician, a burlesque dancer, a coke addict, a wild young denizen of the Lower East Side—aren't wholly false, but they're well chosen ones that bolster her new persona, one that has wholly subsumed the girl formerly known as Stefani Joanne Angelina Germanotta, the girl who today only answers to Lady Gaga. "I think she's got this Prince thing [happening now]," her former producer Rob Fusari said to the *New York Post*. "It's changed. She's Gaga now."

"When she says in interviews, 'I live and breathe fashion'— she may be fooling other people, but she's not fooling me," says Jon Sheldrick, a moon-faced twenty-four-year-old who knew her at New York University and whose friends were members of the Stefani Germanotta Band. "I don't mean to sound demeaning," he continues, "but she was really normal." (Because this is really one of the meanest things one art-school kid could say about another.) Sheldrick, it should be noted, is wearing jeans and a T-shirt.

"She wasn't super-outspoken or into really edgy clothes," he says. "She was wearing T-shirts and sweatpants and shit. She was not a misfit."

"She was a very suburban, friendly, social party girl," said a former dorm-mate, who was friends with the boys in Stefani's then–jam band. "There was nothing that would tip you off that she had this Warhol-esque 'new art' extremism."

"Her 'crazy' outfit," another friend recalled for the same *Post* story, "was putting suspenders on her jeans."

While the crafting and controlling of one's creation myth is hardly new—it's an American art form, from P. T. Barnum to Henry Ford to the Kennedys to Bob Dylan—what's remarkable about Lady Gaga is that she's the first star born in and of the Internet age to master this difficult art.

She's also the first pop star to truly understand, even at this late date, how to exploit, in the best possible sense, the reach of the Web and social media. In November 2009, *Forbes* magazine stated, "Lady Gaga isn't the music industry's new Madonna. She's its new business model."

Gaga (or, most likely, a member of her team) is constantly communicating with her fans via Facebook and Twitter, and when she says something, the response can be seismic. When she announced the debut of her single "Bad Romance" at Alexander McQueen's spring/summer 2010 collection, the site that was streaming the McQueen show crashed almost immediately. Nearly four million people follow her on Twitter. She debuts her videos on YouTube; in March 2010, she became the first artist in history to generate one billion hits, and by February, her album *The Fame* went diamond, having sold ten million copies worldwide. In 2009, she was the most downloaded artist in UK chart history, and was, inexplicably, second only to the Black Eyed Peas as the most downloaded artist on iTunes. It's no exaggeration to say that her closest living relative in this regard might be another global phenomenon who was also little known just a few years ago, and whose peerless use of the Web and social networking largely helped get him to the White House.

Perhaps she had help from her father, Joe, a burly, tough Italian-American who himself was an Internet entrepreneur back in the mid-eighties, when few people had any idea what was coming. He made his fortune with a company called Guest-WiFi, which provides wireless service to hotels. Like him, she's been described as not necessarily book-smart but intuitively business-minded, excellent at reading people. She knew from a very early age that she wanted to be a performer; perhaps she always had the long view in mind.

"I'm a friend of hers on Facebook still; she still has her original profile up," says Seth Kallen, a fellow musician at NYU. "She only has, like, four hundred friends. At first it was like, half her Lady Gaga pictures and half normal pictures. I remember having a sort of revelation—'Wait a minute, she's getting extremely famous.' And I checked out her Facebook profile, and the normal pictures disappeared."

CREATION MYTH

13

There is very little to be found of the young Stefani Germanotta on the Web. There's one clip of her on MTV's now-defunct practical joke show *Boiling Points,* a sort of postmodern *Candid Camera* in which unsuspecting people in everyday situations are provoked until they lose their temper. In Stefani's episode, she's sitting alone at Bari, a generically upscale coffee shop near her NYU campus. She's wearing a strapless black cotton sundress and flip-flops, her long black hair pulled up in a ponytail, black eyeliner and nude lipgloss her only makeup. She looks utterly unremarkable.

Like two other lone diners, she gets up to take a call on her cell phone, and when she returns, her food is gone. When she asks the waitress if she can have her salad back—"It wasn't even eaten!"—the waitress returns her food with a dirty napkin and a balled up piece of plastic on top of it. The other two unwitting contestants are equally shocked, but guess who loses her temper first?

"Who puts that in their mouth?" Stefani asks the waitress. "Would you put that in your mouth? It has shit all over it. Clearly you would, because you're just fucked up."

Stefani lost; for keeping their cool, the other two won $100.

In her high school yearbook, she claims to have been on *The Sopranos.* She spent her teen years auditioning for talent scouts, and tried out for *Rent* when it was still on Broadway. She says her mother kept telling her to slow down when she was in high school. "But," Gaga says, "I was getting hungrier and hungrier."

She was a student at the Convent of the Sacred Heart on East 91st Street. It's an exclusive, all-girls Catholic school set in two converted mansions; alumni include Paris and Nicky Hilton, Gloria Vanderbilt, and Caroline Kennedy. Students begin learning French and Spanish in kindergarten; in eighth grade, they can take Mandarin. Tuition for the 2009–2010 school year is $33,985, and the school's foremost goal, as stated on its website, is to "educate to a personal and active faith in God."

Of her time at Sacred Heart, Gaga has said that she felt like "a freak," that she didn't fit in. But photos from this time show a fresh-faced girl, perpetually smiling, surrounded by other, perpetually smiling young girls. They all look like they're part of the same well-adjusted, uptown tribe: long groomed hair, age-appropriate makeup, jeans and T-shirts and sweaters for day, strapless gowns and pearl chokers at high school dances.

"Stefani was always part of school plays and musicals," said a former Sacred Heart classmate. "She had a core group of friends who she remains close with to this day. She was a good student and wore her uniform mostly to dress code. She liked boys a lot, but her singing and her passion for the arts was number one for her. You could pick Stefani's voice out from others during Mass or a prize-day ceremony. She was always wanting to be an actress or a singer, and it was plain to see that she was going to be a star."

The few early, substantial clips of Stefani that exist on YouTube are performances. There's a now-famous one of her at an NYU talent show, seated behind a piano in a strapless green dress with long, filmy white panels, barefoot. She's singing two very earnest, Norah Jones–sounding ballads. There's another, much earlier one, of her at the Bitter End, a deeply uncool space that evokes all the danger of a suburban rec room. Here, she's a teenager with a little baby fat, in a one-shouldered sweatshirt, *Flashdance*-style, exposing a meridian of belly. She's working out, with swagger and a smirk and smudgy black eyeliner, an early version of "Hollywood." She introduces everyone on stage as "the Stefani Germanotta Band," impatiently looks over at her noodling guitarist, and finally begins. She is probably all of sixteen. "Listen," she growls, full of force and verve, "I've got the sickest ambition."

And another clip, shortly after she got her first record deal—"I didn't sign with Sony, I signed with Island Def Jam," she somewhat haughtily corrects the emcee—sitting behind the piano in a pink minidress and go-go boots. Here, too, she looks thoroughly pedestrian in her long black hair and thick bangs, but she has already started to go by Lady Gaga; this song, called "Wonderful," is another ballad. Her vocals at this point are far more reminiscent of Christina Aguilera—she's begun studying with Aguilera's vocal coach—and this song, sonically and thematically, is very similar to Aguilera's 2002 self-empowerment piano-ballad "Beautiful." ("Wonderful" will eventually go to future *American Idol* contestant Adam Lambert, himself a performer given to high theatricality and heavy eye makeup.)

These clips are evidence of Gaga's undeniable talent; they prove that she's the real deal when it comes to musicianship, vocal ability, and commanding stage presence. Maybe she allows them to live because she cannot legally take them down, but maybe she allows them to live to show that she's nobody's puppet: not a creature of Auto-Tune (the software that manipulates off-key vocals into soulless perfection); not a lip-synching glitter queen, but a true artist with a voice and a vision. Also, in that last clip, she does claim to own a blow-up doll. "And I make love to it every night," she says. So there are glimmers of the witty provocateur she will become.

To her devotees, however, there's not much disconnect between the suburban-looking Stefani Germanotta and the dance-pop dominatrix Lady Gaga, and those who claim there is are quickly mocked for their overall naïveté. And this, too, is probably generational; her younger fans came of age when reality TV and DVD bonus tracks and the Internet exposed most of the sausage-making involved in attaining and retaining modern celebrity. There's not much mystery left anymore, but Gaga, so far, is working both sides of that expertly.

It's hard to think of a recent celebrity who seemed to emerge from nowhere, who's captivated the attention of such wide swaths of people, and about whom next to nothing is known. Her backstory was intentionally limited; you didn't know the details of her childhood, whether she suffered any traumatic domestic episodes, who she was dating, who her friends were. She's not been shot stumbling out of a trendy nightclub or party filled with other young celebrities; she's been able to credibly claim that she's really not of that world, has no real celebrity friends, and has no interest in anything but her art. She's posited herself as none of her peers have: a blank slate, a creature of self-invention, an object of emotional projection and wish-fulfillment. Prince pulled it off, Bowie, too, but both did it before the Internet, and both did it without the warmth Gaga has been able to exude; their mystery seemed born of an essential coldness, a disaffection with the human race. It was totally believable that both belonged to an alien species. Gaga's seems born of genuinely feeling like the misfit she's claimed to be. She seems human.

So it's no surprise that tracks from a 2009-released demo EP called "Red and Blue"—this one sounding like a cross between Avril Lavigne and Alanis Morrissette, more pissed-off mall rat than lovelorn poetess—elicit world-weary debate among the YouTube commentariat.

For example:

"omg this song is so . . . non-perverted!!!! WHAT HAP-PENED LADY GAGA?????!!. . . . maybe she went down the wrong path somewhere."

"8kater, what makes the path she went down 'wrong'? Had she kept down this path, she would never have been known."

"if she made the same songs with the stefani persona do you think she would of sold records? Nope."

"true these are really good, but what shes doing now is heard much more = more sales for the record companies."

"Gaga herself has said that she was bored with being this angry white girl crooning and would have walked out on her performances. So when she was doing this she was selling out because she didn't really like it. I'm not sure if she is 100 percent happy with what she's doing now, but I'm sure she's happy that she's being different."

Gaga's own explanation for the yawning gap between then and now perfectly aligns with that last contention. "The way that I perform, people think it's exhibitionist because it's so theatrical," she said in a previously unpublished interview. "But I tell you, there is something in me that I can't help, and that is the girl who got made fun of all those years. And when I went to college, I got rid of her and I started to be something that I thought I was supposed to be. And when I went in with [my producer], he said, 'I don't know, why don't you bring her out?' Everything I tried to erase about myself, he loved. And so here we are."

Here's where the creation myth begins to unravel.

Her friends and fellow classmates at NYU's Tisch School of the Arts, which Gaga attended for only a year, speak mainly to her laserlike focus. They don't really remember who her friends were or what classes she took or which boys she dated or what parties she attended; they remember her working, performing, always hustling. Her NYU classmate Sheldrick recalls first meeting Stefani at the Alphabet Lounge in fall 2005, after his own set. Her opening line: "Hi, I'm Stefani. I'm trying to start a band. We need a guitar player."

Sheldrick was good friends with Calvin Pia and Eli Silverman, already Stefani's recruits. A few days later, on his way to audition for her band, he found himself at the address he'd been given, walking to a set of open sidewalk grates on the Lower East Side's Ludlow Street, descending a metal staircase, then loping through a long, dirty, pipe-lined hallway until he reached a pocket of rooms in the back. He remembers thinking two things: that this below-ground rehearsal space was disgusting, and that they were probably all on the same page musically. He was into jam bands, as were Calvin and Eli. Stefani was conversant, if not proficient.

"If you looked at her, you'd think she was a jam-band chick," Sheldrick says. "She had a heady, grimy vibe to her. I remember we played Phish's 'Down with Disease.' We did some jam on a one-four-five progression kind of thing, and then after playing Phish for like twenty minutes she was like, 'Can we play some of my songs now?'"

Sheldrick yielded. "I'm not the cool police, but I wasn't really feeling it. I would characterize it as female Billy Joel, like, piano rock." Sheldrick opted not to join the band, but would go to the gigs performed first as the Stefani Germanotta Band and then, for a time, as Stefani Live. "I always went to their shows," he says. They were his friends; he wanted to be supportive. "However much I hate the Bitter End—that place blows—I went anyway."

These performances were unadorned and straightforward. "It was all very normal, very singer-songwriter-y," says her NYU friend Kallen, who played on several bills with her yet, with apology, says he doesn't remember all that much. "It was just the Stefani Germanotta Band; she'd have her piano standing up. The band, to be honest—they weren't that great. I always thought she was talented. I'm sure she realized, 'I gotta do something unique.'"

At the same time, her father had asked Joe Vulpis, a producer and engineer who'd worked with Lindsay Lohan, if he'd do his daughter's first demo, which was part of her audition to get into NYU's Tisch School of the Arts—her childhood dream. The two men were friends who'd met through their membership in an Italian-American organization in Manhattan: "It's a private club, like a country club–type place," Vulpis says. "Giuliani's a member. It's real high-class."

Her parents not only encouraged their daughter's ambition, but were so actively involved in her burgeoning career that they seem to be among the first generation of "helicopter parents." The term was introduced in 1990, and refers to parents who are overly invested, very protective. Joe would use his business connections to get his teenage daughter auditions with executives in the music industry; her mom, Cynthia, would escort young Stefani to nightclubs, beseeching them to allow her underage daughter to perform; they'd carry her gear, call upon extended family to show up for gigs. They knew she had a shot, was very gifted, though the self-generated myth that she'd learned to play the piano at age four—by ear—is another fabrication, as she told one of the very first people to interview her. (That person wishes to go unnamed.)

"When I was four, my mom sent me to a piano teacher—she came to the house—[and] I really hated it," Gaga said. "I didn't want to learn how to read music, or practice." Her mother, she recalled, "wanted me to be a cultured young woman. She would make me sit at the piano for two hours. So I could just sit there, or I could play."

Gaga did go on to say that she then learned largely by ear, because that was the way she wanted to, and that she was a born exhibitionist who demanded constant attention: "We'd be at dinner at a nice restaurant and I would be at the table dancing and using the breadsticks as a baton," she said. "For babysitter interviews, I'd stand between the couches and strip and then I'd jump out naked. At, like, nine. Too old to be doing it."

She thought about acting, too, and as she got older, her parents allowed her to pursue it on the weekends. But music was really her thing.

"I wrote my first song when I was thirteen," Gaga said. "It was called 'To Love Again.' What a thirteen-year-old knows about love is hilarious." She was fourteen when she began playing in downtown nightclubs. (Her six-years-younger sister, Natali, also expressed an interest in music; Gaga's former producer, Rob Fusari, remembers being at dinners at the Germanottas' massive apartment on the Upper West Side and picking up on tension between the two siblings. "I could tell that itch was starting," Fusari says. "Her little sister would sit at the piano and want to show Stefani some of the things she was playing, and Stef would be like, 'This is my thing. Don't invade my territory.'")

Vulpis, Joe Germonatta's producer friend, had seen the Stefani Germanotta Band perform. He was dubious: "The band," he says, "I wasn't too fond of. But, you know, that's what we— that's what we were gifted with." Plus, he liked Joe and thought Stefani had some talent. He and Stefani worked together for five or six months.

"She really wanted to be the bad girl rocker," Vulpis says. They'd do "stripped-down rock, bad-girl rock, big power ballads, jazz standards." She covered torch songs like "Someone to Watch Over Me" and Nat King Cole's "Orange Colored Sky."

When playing live with the band, Stefani tended toward the jammier stuff. She often performed a song called "Purple Monkey," which, she said, was about "smoking weed, taking toke and hallucinating." An olive branch to her Phish-loving cohorts, perhaps? None of her bandmates remembers her as a drug-user or heavy drinker; she was too ambitious for that.

"It had a really bluesy chorus," she said, "and I'd beat on the piano and everyone would go crazy." Columbia Records had people at that show, she said, scouting her. They were per-plexed.

The problem, they told her: " 'We get the voice, but we don't get the music.' " She added, "I had no fucking idea who I was. I had no clue."

Vulpis's recollection is different: "Stefani always knew what she wanted—maybe not right away, but she knew if she didn't like something, to fix it," he says. "She was definitely in charge."

Kallen remembers Calvin Pia coming up to him with an interesting bit of news. "He said, 'We all got kicked out of the Stefani Germanotta Band because she wants to do this new thing. She's Lady Gaga.' "

Musician Wendy Starland first met Gaga, then Stefani, back in 2006, when Stefani was working as an intern for the re-nowned producer Irwin Robinson at Famous Music Publishing, which was a subsidiary of MTV's parent company Viacom (in 2007, Sony/ATV Music Publishing bought the company, then ranked among the industry's Top 10). Famous Music was lo-cated in a Midtown office building, on Broadway, not far from the famed Brill Building, home to Phil Spector, Carole King, Burt Bacharach, and many other American pop powerhouses.

Starland was in the office all the time; Stefani was Robinson's coffee fetcher and phone answerer.

Stefani, Wendy says, would compliment her profusely, raving about her songwriting abilities as she put Starland's press packets together. "There was a song of mine called 'Stolen Love,'" Starland recalls, "and she said, 'I play it over and over again; it meant a lot to me.' Like, 'I love your music.' She's very smart. She knows about people; she knows how to handle people. She's great at getting her way."

Starland is sitting in a booth at the upscale-yet-casual Coffee Shop on Union Square, where she has been taking meetings with producers for the past five hours. A well-groomed girl with fair skin, no makeup, and long, wavy black hair, she looks like a more conventionally pretty Minnie Driver. She is dressed very conservatively, in a cream-colored Talbots-style V-neck sweater and plain, pale pink pants. To look at her, you would never guess that she was in the music industry. She seems more like a banker, or a real estate broker. She ejects herself from the booth about three times over five hours in order to go to the bathroom and calm down; talking about Gaga, even now, makes her very uneasy. "I'm so nervous," she says. "[But] this is all the truth."

When she met Stefani at Famous Music, Starland—whose own poppy, romantic sound is reminiscent of Natasha Bedingfield—was also working as a scout for the New Jersey–based producer Fusari, who'd produced number one hits for Will Smith, Destiny's Child, Whitney Houston, and Jessica Simpson. Fusari had made enough money for enough people that he was now in a rare position: If he could discover someone, mold and shape them and sell them to a label, he stood to make a substantial profit off his discovery.

Fusari had tasked Starland with finding a girl who was twenty-five years old or younger, who, in his words, "could be the lead singer of the Strokes"—a female version of that band's rumpled, woozy front man Julian Casablancas. Stefani was not that. But when Starland shared a bill with her in June of 2006 at another generic, un–rock 'n' roll venue called the Cutting Room, on 24th Street in Manhattan's Flatiron District, she knew that Stefani definitely had *something,* which was Fusari's number one criterion.

"He said, 'She doesn't have to be drop-dead gorgeous, she doesn't have to even have the best talent in the world,'" Starland recalls. "'The necessary requirements are: You can't take your eyes off of her.'"

For her part, Stefani made sure that Starland would see her performance: "I got to the venue early to sound check," Starland recalls, "and she came up to me and was like, 'You remember me, Stefani? I was the intern for Irwin Robinson? We're going to be performing tonight, you should come check it out.'"

Starland remembers her train of thought while watching Stefani at the piano: The songs need polishing. The band has to go. She sounds way too much like Fiona Apple. What is this girl *wearing*? She looks like she's ready to Jazzercize. This performance is beautiful. This girl has guts.

"After the show," says Starland, "I took her by the wrist and said to her, 'I'm about to change your life.' It was that cinematic."

CREATION MYTH

♦ ♦ ♦

The girls went outside and Starland dialed Fusari; Stefani's bandmate/boyfriend was around somewhere, but Starland says he was so nondescript she can't recall much about him. "Stefani wore the pants in that relationship," says Starland. "I was like, 'Your girlfriend has huge balls and she's really got something,' and he was like, 'Yeah, she does.'" A few minutes after that exchange, Starland told Stefani she'd have to ditch the band, which meant ditching the boyfriend. "She doesn't bat an eye," Starland says. "Trust me, the boyfriend was gone a week later."

Gaga remembered that night much the same way: "Wendy Starland came up to me and says, 'Holy fucking shit, you have elephant balls for a chick!' She sinks her fingers into my arm and pulls me outside and looks me dead in the eye and says, 'I'm about to change your life.' And she calls up Rob and says, 'I've found her.'"

"This is 2006, the year record sales were tanking," says Brendan Sullivan, a New York City DJ who would befriend Gaga a few months later. "This is the year when no one wanted to hear anything 'still'—it's the Strokes and Interpol and everything is really fuzzed out, and the Killers are so big. Everything has a funk pedal. But when you hear Gaga, the notes are crystal clear. She really stood out. It was refreshing to hear her."

Fusari, meanwhile, had been roused from a sound sleep. "He said, 'Why are you waking me up?'" says Starland. "And I said, 'I found the girl. Trust me. We're gonna change her style, we're gonna write all new songs, we're gonna get a whole new band, and produce her totally differently.'"

Fusari went to Stefani's website, took a look and a listen while Starland held the line, and got further incensed. "He said, 'Wendy, this is not going to happen. Don't waste my time.' And I said, 'Don't listen to these recordings, it's about who she is live.' Then, according to Starland, Fusari expressed concern about Stefani's look; Starland kept pushing. "Stefani's standing right there," she says. "She hears this." Throughout all the criticism, the future Gaga remained unfazed. "She just wants to get to Rob."

Wendy put Stefani on the phone.

"That," she says, "was my first mistake." Had she only gotten something in writing, she says, that established herself as more than a freelance talent scout, she would have had so much more leverage down the line, when she found herself no longer needed.

At Starland's urging, Fusari checked out Stefani's next gig a few weeks later. "It was some shitty little club on First or Second Avenue, some hole in the wall, same sucky band," Starland says. After the set, Fusari called Starland. "Wendy," he said, "honestly, are you kidding me? Are you fucking *kidding* me?"

Stefani didn't speak to Fusari at all that night, but she saw him leave right after the set and knew what that meant. Stefani called Starland "incessantly," she says. "I was like, 'Don't worry.' She's panicked. Very concerned." Starland says that Stefani had the absolute right reaction. "She wasn't crazy at all. It was 100 percent slipping out of her grasp."

Stefani was also running out of time: Nine months prior, her father had allowed her to drop out of college to pursue a record deal, and if it didn't happen within his time frame, back to college she went. She'd gotten a tiny, three-hundred-square-foot apartment on the Lower East Side, a clear downgrade from her parents' luxurious apartment in a doorman building on the Upper West Side. She was living alone, but she hated to be alone. The façade of her parents' building is nothing special; it looks like an anonymous, bland, cream-colored postwar structure. Those who have been inside say the apartment is warm but lavish, with two or possibly three floors. Stefani and her sister, Natali, had their own bedrooms upstairs. The focal point of the living room was an oil painting of the family, done when the girls were very young, that hung over the mantel. From her parents' place on a very quiet uptown sidestreet, Stefani was within walking distance of Lincoln Center, the Metropolitan Museum of Art, and Central Park, in a neighborhood where everything was very clean, very orderly, very expensive, and very safe.

She'd left that homogeneous safety zone for life eighty blocks downtown, which doesn't sound so far away but is the polar opposite of uptown. Downtown New York City is a mash-up of cultures, the very rich and the very poor, the corporate and the counterculture. She was toggling two different worlds and was increasingly at loose ends. She'd sometimes spend the night sleeping in her old bedroom uptown, where, unlike on the dirty, sketchy Lower East Side, there was little crime and no street noise. She could regress and retreat.

Two weeks after the gig, Fusari agreed to have one meeting with Stefani.

TWO

BECOMING GAGA

*I*n early 2006, Stephani took the bus from New York's Port Authority out to Parsippany, New Jersey, where Fusari lives and works; his tiny studio is on the same property as his house and has an open-plan feel; he tends to leave it unlocked, so musicians can come and go as they please. It's tricked out with modernist furniture, has a very sixties mod vibe. As Fusari was approaching the bus stop where he'd agreed to pick Stefani up, he saw a small, chunky girl in a pizza place. She looked like she was asking for directions.

"That could be her," he remembers thinking. "But I hope it's not."

He vividly remembers what she was wearing: "It was, like, a mix of three different eras," he says. "She had on leggings and some strange cut-up shirt and a hat that looked like it was right out of Prince's *Purple Rain*." Fusari's vision was to find a modern-day Chrissie Hynde: a girl who, in his words, was "pretty, but not really pretty," skinny and tough, possessed of a swaggering sexuality that would read as traditionally male but be subversively female.

To him, Stefani was a mess. He was afraid the outward appearance reflected inner chaos: that this was a girl with no taste, no vision, no talent. She presented as just another delusional girl with a dream. Good manners stopped him from telling her to turn around and go home.

"In my mind," he says today, "I was done."

Tommy Kafafian, a kind, if spacey, twenty-six-year-old studio musician who was working with Fusari, had tagged along, and says they only ever stopped in the pizza place because he was starving and begged Fusari to let him grab a slice. He remembers seeing Stefani and thinking to himself, *Wow!* In a good way.

"There was this cute chick with long black hair and white stockings," he says today, on the phone from Atlanta, Georgia, where he's "in the best rock 'n' roll band of all time," hoping to tour the moon: "I want to be the first."

Back to his meeting with Stefani: "I went in for a slice of pizza, and that's where I met her. [On] Planet Earth. She just manifested into my reality." Fusari was waiting in the car; Stefani was skittish. Here was this trippy kid telling her to come with him, he was her ride, the guy she was really meeting was waiting for her outside in a car.

"She kind of looked a little weird, like she was afraid," Kafafian recalls. "I go, 'Don't be scared, it's cool.' She got in the car, and we went to the studio."

Fusari could not get over her appearance. "She looked like something out of *GoodFellas*," he says. "She was a little overweight. She looked like she was ready to make pasta at any minute." They made small talk, he says, "the usual BS." He'd heard some of her stuff on MySpace: "It sounded like a Gwen Stefani cover band." He was unimpressed. He asked her to play something.

"I got, like—I tell you, it was ten seconds in, she was play-ing 'Hollywood'"—that faux-blues-y song from her Bitter End days, in which she sang about having "the sickest ambition"—"and I'm like, 'Oh my God.' I'm thinking to myself, 'If I don't get this, I'm going to be so disappointed. My mind went right to business; I couldn't even hear the song. I'm sitting in back of her and I'm texting my management, like, 'I need a contract. Immediately.'"

Starland, though she was not in the studio that day, recalls Fusari's reaction differently. "Once he heard her live in the studio, he and I conversed a lot more about whether he was going to do this," she says. "He said to me, 'It's good, but . . .' The amount of work it takes to start from scratch is inordinate. So even though he says to the newspapers now, 'I knew within five seconds'—not true."

Stefani, meanwhile, told Fusari she was a complete novice, had no knowledge of the way the music industry worked. "I found out, later, that she really *had* shopped to most labels," he says. She had left out the numerous auditions she'd been on as a teenager, ones with major industry players, arranged by her father. "It was just funny, you know, to start uncovering the real story."

Once Fusari agreed to sign Stefani to a production deal, he got a clearer idea of who he was dealing with. Stefani was demanding an 80-20 deal: 80 percent of the monies would go to her, 20 percent to Fusari. It was beyond ballsy, especially given that this was a nineteen-year-old unknown who very badly needed a producer like Fusari, with his résumé and connec-tions. The negotiations were so contentious that Fusari began reconsidering the entire signing; maybe it would be easier to find someone else, cut ties now.

"She was freaking out," says Starland, "very nervous that it wouldn't go through. When it comes to negotiating, Rob is very emotional. He did not like the structure of the deal. He felt he was bringing more to the table and tried to take a really big percentage. That's when her father stepped in."

In the end, after a month of negotiations between lawyers, both parties came to terms: 40 percent went to Stefani, 40 percent to her father, and 20 percent to Fusari under the banner of a limited liability company called "Team Love Child."

"Gaga's dad, with his history in telecom—he knows not to get into a contract you can't get out of," says her friend Brendan Sullivan. "I think that's why the Team Love Child split is how it is. The example I would give is the iPhone: If you want the iPhone, you have to get into a contract with AT&T, but you don't have to get into a lifetime contract with AT&T. I think if Rob Fusari were her producer forever, we wouldn't have great music. With Rob, she came out with some of the least exciting singles on *The Fame:* 'Beautiful, Dirty, Rich,' 'Disco Heaven,' which was a B-side, 'Boys Boys Boys.' You have to wonder what [she went] through to write what came afterwards."

Stefani has spoken of her father's approval meaning so much to her that, even if his is the lone voice, it's enough to cause dramatic shifts in her behavior. She's famously said that the only comment he ever made about her partying—"You're fucking up, kid"—was the catalyst for her to stop using cocaine. "He is my hero," she told the journalist Touré during an interview with *Fuse* in 2009.

Her mother, Cynthia, is described by those who know her as a beautiful, cultured, kind woman. She is short and a natural brunette, like her daughter. She was a huge influence on the young Stefani's tastes. "My mom would have fashion-fun with me," Gaga has said. "She'd dress me in neon leggings and oversized shirts. I had this killer visor—like a casino-green vinyl visor—with lights that would flash. I wore it to a roller-skating party once." She also said she used to get overdressed for school: "I would do Marilyn Monroe curls," she recalled. "To be honest, I thought I looked great. But I got made fun of. I used to wear really tight everything under my school uniform— I'd get in trouble for V-necks and hooker boots. I look back now at photos and laugh."

Though she's given equal weight to both parents, and has said that she "worships" them, of the two, her father seems to be the dominant force in her life. In the January 2010 issue of *Elle,* she told journalist Miranda Purves that she didn't have a boyfriend at the moment, but that it was OK: "I'm married to my dad."

Paul Rizzo, who is the co-owner of the Bitter End and had been booking Stefani since she was a teenager, recalls Joe "always, always" accompanying his daughter to gigs. "Because she was young," Rizzo says. "He might have even been driving her down at the time. He was carrying her keyboards for her. He was very supportive. Even when she changed into Lady Gaga—I don't even think he got it at first, but he was never against it. They fed the talent. She had a good strong family unit."

Later, when she had her first major New York gig at Terminal 5, Rizzo recalls Joe reaching out to another co-owner of the Bitter End, Kenny Gorka, for "certain advice about the business." Joe has largely quit working in the tech sector to become a full-time music manager; aside from his daughter, he has two other clients, in another company formed with Gaga, Mermaid Music, LLC, in which both are equal business partners.

"I was at her parents' house [in February 2008] and Gaga was giving her dad shit—he hadn't done a bunch of things," says Brendan Sullivan. "She was like, 'What the hell have you been doing?' He goes"—jokingly, says Sullivan—"'Look, I'm a big-time record producer now, I've got three acts I'm working with here!'"

She is, however, her father's daughter, stubborn and tough, and she's never followed a dictate she herself did not agree with. One friend remembers Stefani hanging out at her place before a meeting with Sony, wearing tights with her underpants on the outside. Her dad, Stefani said, told her that she looked like "a fucking slut!" and she laughed that off, though it seemed she was actually hurt. She acted as though she was more alarmed to realize that she'd forgotten to shave her knees.

On Joe's end, it's possible he was equally afraid that his daughter's appearance would undermine her credibility. "Their relationship definitely improved as she made more money," says a source. "That helped substantially. She's always been trying to get his approval. I don't know that it's healthy. As soon as she started earning money, he said something to her like 'What man wouldn't want you now that you're becoming so successful?'"

Of late, his daughter has taken to telling interviewers that she will always put her career before a man, because a career won't roll over in bed one morning and tell you it doesn't love you anymore.

By April 2006, Stefani and Fusari had fully set to work on crafting a sound. Stefani was committed to being a serious singer-songwriter. Fusari thought that idea wasn't of-the-moment, let alone forward-thinking. He'd just read a piece in the *New York Times*, "talking about women in rock, and how it was getting very difficult for women to break through in that genre, how Nelly Furtado had moved into more of a dance thing."

He told Stefani that this was the future, the way to go. "I was like, 'Look, I think we might not be going in the right direction.' This wasn't something kids could relate to. And she was like, 'No, I like what I'm doing. I'm not changing.'"

"She was really more earthy and hippie and stuff," says Kafafian, who was writing with her at the time. "She was kind of into the jam band scene. She wrote cool songs and it was kind of like Bob Dylan." "Brown Eyes" and "Blueberry Kisses" were among the fifty written during this time, he says. They were inspired, says Starland, by Fusari.

"Rob wanted to do a more modern sound," Kafafian says. "He didn't want to make an organic record, like I wanted. Everybody's fighting. They're eating each other."

Fusari insisted on dance music—according to him and Kafafian. Another source says the stuff they were recording at this time sounded like her high school and college material, like Michelle Branch and Avril Lavigne, half piano-driven balladry, half bratty teen-girl complaint-rock. Fusari won: Stefani would be working toward a more sugary, dance-oriented sound—the airy confections that were the hallmark of Euro-pop superproducer-songwriters such as Max Martin, the thirty-nine-year-old Swede behind some of the catchiest, most ear-wormy songs of the past fifteen years, including the Backstreet Boys' "As Long as You Love Me" and Kelly Clarkson's "Since U Been Gone."

Stefani—a huge fan of Britney Spears, for whom Martin had written ". . . Baby One More Time," Britney's first-ever hit—was vociferously against the idea. She may not have known what was cool, but she knew what wasn't, even if she'd once cried outside of *TRL* after seeing Britney in person as a high schooler. And she was genuinely a fan of serious artists who wrote their own stuff: She'd been raised on Bruce Springsteen, Billy Joel, the Beatles. She wanted to be earnest and heartfelt.

Still, there was another problem, one that was far more sensitive: Stefani didn't have the ready-made looks of an American pop star in waiting. Fusari and Starland didn't think she could pull off the girl-at-a-piano thing, because, as Starland explains, not a bit uncharitably, you have to be very, very pretty to do that (think Norah Jones, Fiona Apple, Tori Amos).

These discussions, Starland says, happened openly among the three of them. Stefani remained stoic and practical. She would avoid hanging out at Starland's place: "I know that the pressure on her to [lose weight] was very high," Starland says. "She'd come over to my house all the time, and I had Pringles and Hostess cupcakes—I eat very poorly—and she'd be like, 'Oh God, I don't want to deal with this. This is the worst place for me to be.'" But she'd eat that stuff anyway. Her father bought her a membership at the Reebok Sports Club on the Upper West Side and she started hitting the gym regularly. She dropped fifteen pounds.

"I was saying, 'We can do something theatrical so it's not the attention on her looks,'" Starland recalls. "She talked about it on her own, too. She was actively involved; she was like, 'I know that my look is untraditional, and that I'm not the classic beauty, so we have to do other things.' Really pragmatic. That wasn't a process where I felt like she was hurt in any way. She was going to do whatever it took to become famous."

So dance music became the obvious route, but the idea was to sound a bit more sophisticated and European discotheque-y, a hybrid of hot and cold, like Kylie Minogue's "Can't Get You Out of My Head" or Goldfrapp's slinky, synth-y "Number 1": the contrast of breathy, detached vocals over sexed-up, syncopated beats. "I said, 'I'll sit at the drum machine, you sit at the piano,'" Fusari says of their initial experiment. "What the hell? We don't have to use it."

"The first few songs weren't her sound," Starland says. "I really want to credit Rob with devising . . ." She pauses. "I might have talked about creating a focus more on her body than her face, and because of that, dance seemed like a very natural way for her to go."

That initial experiment with dance tracks, Fusari says, was "the lightbulb moment. Everything just started to make sense. But we didn't have the name yet."

Meanwhile, Stefani was also learning how to navigate the Lower East Side. Ever since the 1980s, the neighborhood, right below the aesthetically similar East Village and right above Chinatown, had been home to the city's vanguard in art and debauchery. Much like today, the East Village and Lower East Side in the eighties overlapped; Keith Haring did a one-night show on St. Mark's Place in the East Village in 1980, and shortly after came the Fun Gallery, two blocks over on East 10th Street, where kids and the curious would go to watch break-dancers and hear hip-hop and look at graffiti sprayed on the walls. Also good for music, dancing, and general troublemaking were the Mudd Club, CBGB (which opened in 1973), and ABC No Rio, a collective space for artists and activists on Rivington Street that still hosts everyone from silkscreeners to anarchists. Jean-Michel Basquiat was there then, too, crossing paths with Andy Warhol and dating a very young Madonna.

In the early-to-mid 1990s, the Lower East Side became just gentrified enough to attract kids from Columbia University and NYU looking to slum it and likely score some really powerful heroin. Ludlow Street was becoming a main artery, with the opening of the venerable dive bar/art space Max Fish; a few doors down was the Alleged Gallery, which showed outsider art and exhibits of skateboard decks, and kept a back room for visiting artists to crash on the floor. (Its founder, Aaron Rose, would later be immortalized as a caddish young playboy on *Gossip Girl,* which one season later featured Lady Gaga in a cameo, performing "Bad Romance" at a school dance.) Cult bands like Jonathan Fire*Eater, which would spawn the more successful Walkmen, were living and playing down there, as was a very young Beck, who could often be found playing coffee shops on Avenue A.

By 2006 the Lower East Side had long been transmogrified into something of a theme park for hipsters. Tourists found their way to Max Fish via Lonely Planet guidebooks, and stars like Jude Law were investors in the infamous grown-up sex house the Box. Famed restauranteur Keith McNally opened Schiller's, a shabby, sophistiated brasserie serving the likes of Karl Lagerfeld and inspiring the locus of the action in Richard Price's best-selling 2008 novel, *Lush Life.* The neighborhood is so well branded that an artist like Santigold can release a song called "L.E.S. Artistes," and not only will it become a hit, but almost everyone who hears it will know what L.E.S. stands for. By the time Stefani took up residence there, the Lower East Side was almost as safe as the Upper West Side, if filthier. But that's part of the appeal, and this Lower East Side was still where all the cool kids were. Members of the Strokes, Interpol, and Yeah Yeah Yeahs ran around down there; the city's best music venues, like the Mercury Lounge and the Bowery Ballroom, were there; it was where A&R people scouted new talent, fashion editors sourced trends, and where the bulk of the city's most-read art and music bloggers lived and worked.

"That period of my life," Gaga has said, "was about me trying to be cool, being the queen of a very small scene, getting my picture taken, dating the hottest bartender. Bartenders are like movie stars down there." (As absurd as that may sound, she's right.) "On the Lower East Side, being Queen of the Scene is like being the queen of two blocks. But it got me in magazines, and it got Interscope"—her future record label—"interested."

She found a place at 176 Stanton Street, and this was the tiny one-bedroom walk-up that was her part-time home when not decamped with her parents. (She didn't have a day job; her much-talked-about stint waitressing was during her sopho-more to senior years in high school.) On the Lower East Side, too, she made quite the impression: One of her neighbors says that, not long after he moved in, his sister asked him if he knew that "there was a prostitute that lives in the building."

Her neighbor was totally flummoxed; Stanton Street, like the bulk of the Lower East Side, was mainly inhabited by young scenesters and professionals. "I was like, 'What are you talking about?' She said, 'I saw this girl stumbling up the stairs at, like, four A.M., wearing, like, nothing, and she was drunk.' And I just remember thinking, 'Oh, great. What a scummy building I live in now.'"

Stefani would spend her days composing and demo-ing at 176 Stanton; her place was sparsely decorated with a futon, a queen-sized mattress, and a record player from Urban Outfit-ters. She had a picture of David Bowie over her bed and she'd sit at her kitchen counter with her keyboard and her laptop, working out songs.

"She had a bare-ass apartment," says her friend Brendan Sullivan, who would go on to work as her DJ. "It just had turntables, a synth, and a couch. It was like a monk's cell—just for work and study."

Stefani was running around in leotards and go-go boots, stumbling up the stairs at four in the morning, but at heart she was an extremely hard worker who kept to herself. Those who knew her during this time and those who knew her once she'd achieved global fame describe her in very similar terms: a girl with insane levels of charisma, who outwardly seemed very popular and self-possessed, but who was actually very difficult to get to know. In this way, perhaps Gaga's description of herself as an alienated teenager, the high school "freak" who never fit in, may not be all that far from the truth. It's possible, after all, to be both popular and alienated. Just watch *Rebel Without a Cause* or *Heathers* or *Gossip Girl*.

In any event, it was the other tenants who caused problems, once dramatically, with Stefani. Her neighbor says that, at one point, some kids who lived in the building "jimmied the lock and broke into her apartment, saw her in the shower—it was a big thing. They all got arrested." Another neighbor happened to be a cop, and he helped make the arrest.

Recently, her old neighbor got a text from that cop, who wrote, "Remember that girl whose apartment was broken into? Stefani? She was a musician and now she's Lady Gaga." It took her old neighbor a while, he says, to believe it. Today, he realizes that the timing of her move out of 176 Stanton—to L.A.— had nothing to do with the break-in, as he'd assumed, and everything to do with the record deal to come.

During her time on the Lower East Side, Stefani would head over to local bars like Welcome to the Johnsons and

St. Jerome's, both of which were managed by a reedy peacock of a rock boy named Lüc, who also worked as a bartender. Once she became Gaga, she said he partially inspired "Paparazzi," with the actual paparazzi and her ravenous desire for fame inspiring the other half.

Lüc Carl is well over six feet tall and, with long black hair that sprays up from his crown like an unruly fern, looks like a cross between Russell Brand and Nikki Sixx. He doesn't so much bartend as lope around and drape himself over the bar, staring into space; a customer waits for him to decide if he's up to making the move to serve you. (The bartender as rock star.) Stefani had her eye on him, but also on a burlesque dancer named Lady Starlight, who worked Fridays at St. Jerome's. Starlight was another celebrity in the scene, a sweet girl who worked a tough, heavy-metal look, who had gigs at all the right bars and knew all the right kids and could get into all the right parties. Gaga wanted to be Starlight's friend.

"She was, and is, incredibly focused and motivated about succeeding," says Starlight, who, back in 2007, with her long black hair, heavy bangs, and misguided dress sense, looked like Stefani's twin. (In pictures taken of the two of them, it's hard to figure out who's who.) She vividly recalls their first meeting, back around 2006: "She tipped me," Starlight says. "In my panties."

Stefani got Starlight's number from Lüc and, just as she'd successfully done with Wendy Starland, began courting her as a best friend. "You couldn't help but notice her," says Starlight, who explains that this was not necessarily the best thing. Starlight, who claims to have been born in 1980 but may be ten years older, says that Stefani looked "abrupt and out of place" among the neighborhood's hipster squad. "She wore spandex, some kind of unitard."

Fusari also remembers Stefani working out her look during this time. He was shocked at both its unadulterated poor taste and Stefani's disregard for what anyone else thought. "It started to evolve into this thing. . . . I don't want to say I started to question it, but I would keep my fingers crossed when she'd show up to meetings," Fusari says. "I could never tell what she'd wear. The color schemes would be really tight leopard-print pants with one-foot-tall red pumps. I was like, 'Is this *The Rocky Horror Picture Show*?' Walking down the street with her, honestly, no exaggeration, 90 percent of people would stop in their tracks. You don't expect that in New York City. I'd be like, 'Stef, you gotta walk a little bit ahead of me. People are gonna say I might be with a prostitute. Or a transsexual prostitute.' It wouldn't even faze her."

A friend who met Stefani not long after has a similar recollection: "People would stare," she says. "She [didn't look] as insane as she does now, but she was definitely not the average person walking down the street. She would wear these leotards from American Apparel—it was almost like she had her underwear on over her clothes."

"The big outfit was fishnets and a backless leotard with a chain belt," says her friend Sullivan, who first met Stefani at St. Jerome's, where Lüc bartended, in December 2006. "She'd wear that and high heels and a leather jacket. That was her jam." He recalls her introducing herself as a singer; Sullivan was often spinning at St. Jerome's. Stefani had just begun dating Lüc; Sullivan says Lüc was extremely posses-sive.

That night, Sullivan was paying more attention to Stefani than to his date, who he knew Lüc also had a crush on. Sullivan found that amusing. He and Stefani were bonding over music and performing, and they decided to exchange numbers. That was enough, Sullivan says, to set Lüc off, which he still finds really funny.

First, Sullivan says, he was putting her name in his phone, but she told him not to punch in "Stefani." She told him to use "Gaga." Lüc was already agitated, and then she got a call. "Lüc goes, 'Who's calling you at eleven at night?' and she goes, 'My producer,'" says Sullivan, laughing. Frustrated, Lüc then turned to Sullivan and yelled, 'Stop talking to my girlfriend, man!'"

He and Lüc got into a bit of a typically pathetic Lower East Side pissing match over who was cooler, more connected, had the more desirable partner. At least, Sullivan says, he had the dignity not to brag that his date had once been involved with Moby, and that Moby hated Sullivan, and how cool was it that an internationally famous musician not only knew who he was but actively disliked him.

Lüc, Sullivan thought, had not yet mastered the difficult, nec-essary downtown art of seeming not to care—unlike Sullivan, who would *never* bring up the Moby connection. In an attempt to smooth things over, Sullivan told Lüc that Stefani was hot. "And he responded, 'Island recording artist,'" says Sullivan. He was turned off by all of Lüc's over-compensation.

Lüc aside, Sullivan is still exhilarated by that evening: "So that was the fateful, fateful, awesome meeting that changed my life, and hers, forever," he says. Because that was the night he met the girl who would become Lady Gaga, and he still can't believe he knows someone that famous.

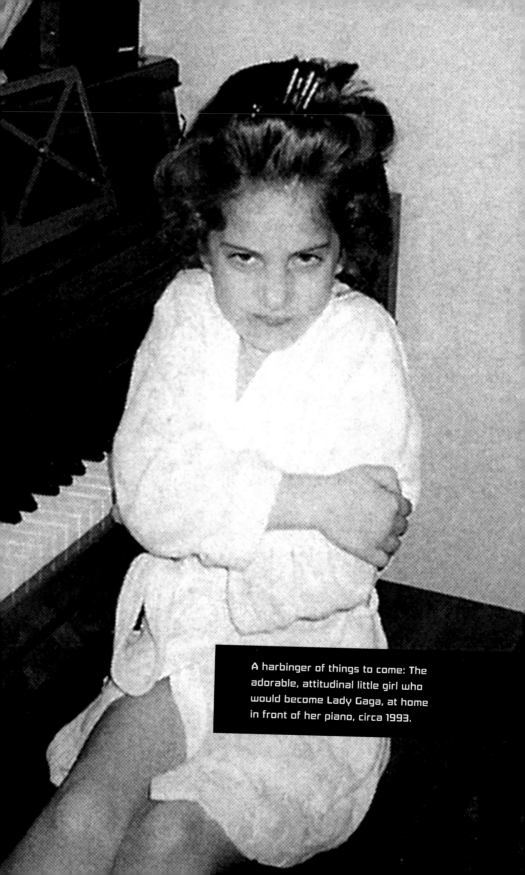

A harbinger of things to come: The adorable, attitudinal little girl who would become Lady Gaga, at home in front of her piano, circa 1993.

A teenage Stefani, looking every bit the well-manicured, popular Upper West Side teen, hugs an unidentified friend in this 2004 Convent of the Sacred Heart yearbook photo.

Name: Stefani Joanne Germanotta
Nickname: Stefi, The Germ
Usually seen: singing
Picture Her: without her midriff showing
Dream: headlining at Madison Square Garden
Reality: Cafe Casa
Male Equivalent: Boy George
Separated at Birth: Britney Spears
Prized Possession: her piano
Pet Peeve: "ordinary" people
Bet you didn't know: she was on *The Sopranos*
Didn't come to reunion: she had an audition

Stefani's senior-year bio, from her yearbook. Remarkable, no?

The self-proclaimed teenage "freak" (bottom, far left), with a gaggle of strikingly normal-looking pals, in another shot from her senior high school yearbook.

The makeover begins: a markedly thinner Stefani, now Lady Gaga, with black hair and white nails, at the 2007 BMI showcase "Who's Next? Writers on the Rise."

A disco-ball bra, green-stain tap pants with a leopard-print waist, and shiny pink shoes: the ever-gestating Lady Gaga shot at her first big break, Lollapalooza, 2007.

Gaga in a traditional Vietnamese hat, flanked by dancers Melissa Emrico and Celine Thubert, leaving the country after performing on the Miss Universe Pageant 2008.

In her version of beachwear—a skullcap and a vintage Prince and the New Power Generation T-shirt, taken on a rehearsal day for the Miss Universe Pageant 2008 in Vietnam.

The bra made it, the tap pants didn't: Lady Gaga onstage at Lollapalooza. Right after this gig, Gaga fired her manager over a record that skipped during this performance.

Looking like a cross between a Japanese anime heroine and a 1970s disco queen, Lady Gaga performs at Perez Hilton's 2008 CMJ bash at New York City's Highline Ballroom.

Madonna may be the most-referenced, but Missing Persons' Dale Bozzio, performing here in 1983, is one of Gaga's most referenced forebears; there are times when the two look indistinguishable . . .

. . . such as here: Gaga references (or rips off, depending on your worldview) the aerodynamic silver minidress, the pink-streaked platinum blond hair, and aggressive stage presence.

Face paint is half the battle: Lady Gaga, in an undated photo, applies her makeup with an uncharacteristically light hand.

Another heavily sourced icon: The late Brit eccentric and McQueen muse Isabella Blow, infamous for her outrageous clothes and love of bizarre headgear.

Gaga in a gorgeous, cloud-like Issy-inspired mask/headdress at Universal Records' Brit Awards party in London, February 2010. (Designer Alexander McQueen, for whom Blow and Gaga were muses, had committed suicide the week before, and Gaga paid homage to him during her performance.)

The post-post-modern glamour of a true 21st-century pop star: The Lady reclines with BlackBerry, fresh coffee, costume jewelry, cash, and an art journal—all the necessities—in a tub in Paris, 2009.

In a hat designed by architect Frank Gehry and a dress by Miuccia Prada, Lady Gaga performs at the 30th anniversary celebration of MOCA (the Museum of Contemporary Art in Los Angeles). Her piano (not seen here) was designed by famed artist Damien Hirst.

THREE

QUEEN OF THE SCENE

Sullivan and Gaga wound up working together, mainly due to the proximity effect. "I was DJing in the bar, her boyfriend was the bartender, he had a bunch of terrible bands that never went anywhere that I'd book at different shows . . . and she was just part of that," he says. "We couldn't help but hang out every single day." Her clique was formed out of equal parts affinity and necessity: Starland was helping with Fusari and a future record deal; Starlight was giving her a crash course in performance art and Lower East Side hipster-ism; Sullivan was a skilled, popular DJ who could help her with bookings.

And soon enough, Gaga was go-go dancing, under Starlight's tutelage, while Sullivan DJ'd at spots like St. Jerome's, Don Hill's, and Luke & Leroy's, three of the most popular bars for the disheveled and disaffected. Once in a while, Gaga would sing; for a friend's birthday party at the Beauty Bar on 14th Street, another cool-kids hangout retrofitted with 1950s-style cone-shaped hairdryers and manicure stations, she popped out of a cake and sang "Happy Birthday, Mr. President" à la Marilyn Monroe. Even then, her friends sensed she was going to make it.

"I used to walk down the street like I was a fucking star," she has said. "I want people to walk around delusional about how great they can be—and then to fight so hard for it every day that the lie becomes the truth."

"The difference" with Gaga, says Sullivan: "She's, like, four-eleven. She's got a really tiny voice. She was not the cutest girl when she was younger. She's used to people ignoring her, basically. But when she gets up on a stage and has a microphone in her hand, she feels for the first time like she's interacting with people in a different way. Rather than people stooping over to listen to her, people are craning their heads forward to see her better. And that's what we talk about when we talk about 'the fame.'"

Lady Starlight was the one who schooled Stefani in bur-lesque, the downtown bar scene, and how to light fires with hairspray. She took Stefani to her favorite underground party, Frock 'n' Roll in Long Island City, thirty minutes away by train, in Queens. Long Island City has, in recent years, become the new Williamsburg, which for a while was the new Lower East Side. Long Island City is home to this generation's starving artists, but it's also home to the more experimental Museum of Modern Art offshoot P.S.1. Matthew Barney has his studio here.

Stefani's assimilation into the scene wasn't going well. She didn't look the part, didn't get all the esoteric references. "You know how it is in those kinds of artsy circles," Starlight told the *New York Post*. "People are a little snooty."

But Stefani kept at it. She auditioned for a burlesque spot at the Slipper Room, a bordello-ish bar/performance space on Orchard and Stanton streets on the Lower East Side.

"I thought she was just a nice crazy girl from Jersey," says proprietor James Habacker, who hired her on the spot after her first audition in 2007. (He, like many of downtown New York's nightlife denizens, has trouble recalling exact dates.) Gaga's day look, he says, was "kind of slutty." He laughs. Habacker, who cuts a dandyish figure in an expertly tailored olive green overcoat and wavy hair chopped to his cheekbones, is sitting in a back room in the basement of his venue; there are two facing sofas, a wet bar, and a huge silver plate on the coffee table sprinkled with cigarette ashes. He remembers her as always being "super-nice to me," very career-minded, very mature. And not a little off.

"She would do some grinding, get down to pasties and a G-string. She was bringing in some interesting and odd elements—I remember some kind of plushie thing," he says, before trailing off. (Plushies are members of a subculture devoted to the pursuit of sex acts with stuffed animals.)

"I was never a stripper, never topless," Gaga has said. "It was rock 'n' roll burlesque."

Fusari thought the burlesque stuff was beneath her and a waste of her time. So, unsurprisingly, did her father.

"It was a strip show," Fusari has said. "I was like, anyone who came to that show didn't come for the music. And it really started to bother her father. I think now he knows it's part of the act, an extreme, 'Alice in Wonderland'–type thing."

For Gaga, though, it was performance, a chance to learn how to lose herself, to push through her own comfort level, to see what worked and what didn't and figure out ways to adjust accordingly, in the moment. It was, to her, art.

QUEEN OF THE SCENE

"She was clearly smart and professional," Habacker adds. "I thought she was great." The other girls, however, did not. "There were complaints," he says. "Like, 'I don't like her attitude,' 'She's rude to me,' 'She's a diva.' She wasn't mean, I think. She was just distant, and a little strange. But if you don't fit in, it makes it difficult."

Though her act was inventive—Gaga performed with those stuffed animals, pasties, and pyro—Habacker, who only hired forty girls for eighty slots a month, let her go after one year. The rancor she engendered with the other girls—no matter who was at fault—was too disruptive. He was doubly impressed with the way she handled her firing. "You know, she didn't fight me on it," he says. "She was like, 'Best of luck to you.' And I think I might have said, 'Don't forget me if you ever get to be a big star.'" Which is what most every dancer at the Slipper Room thought she'd be.

Stefani was commuting nearly every day, working with Fusari in suburban New Jersey and returning to the bacchanalian L.E.S. at night, attempting to penetrate the scene. Both were struggles, professionally and romantically.

Within a month of working with Fusari, says a formerly close friend, Stefani began dating Fusari's session musician, Tommy Kafafian. "He's a very cute guy, a very good songwriter and musician," says the friend. Fusari had produced a record for Kafafian, who was also playing on some of Stefani's tracks. She really fell for him, says her friend. Kafafian felt differently.

"I was the main squeeze at some point," he says. He guesses they dated for "three or four or six months. It was definitely something I was attracted to. But it wasn't like we were in love at all. It was more, like, we'd hang out hours and hours and days on end in the studio, and I'd drive her home to the city."

She spent nearly all her free time recording: "Nothing could take away from the studio," says her friend. "There was a determination."

She was also in search of a new name—everyone agreed that Stefani Germanotta was far too ungainly and had to go. Despite the numerous origin stories—Fusari's claim that it was the result of a misspelled text, Gaga's claim that it was something Fusari said to her while she was playing a Queen B-side ("You're so gaga!" which doesn't sound like something anyone in a remotely cool profession would ever say)—Starland says the name arrived in a far more typical, pedestrian way: a marketing meeting.

"It was a little bit of a group effort," among her, Fusari, Kafafian, and a few others, Starland says. "It wasn't around a table, but it was like, 'Everybody, let's think about what name is going to be marketable.'"

Queen was, in fact, the inspiration point, though Starland says she never knew Stefani to be a big fan. "We talked about Queen and 'Radio Ga Ga,' and someone came up with 'Lady,' and we put it together. Once 'Lady Gaga' came up, we were like, 'If we tell this to Rob, he's not going to even listen to any of the other names—he's going to fall in love with it."

As for Stefani: "She loved it."

She was also very happy with Kafafian, who was around her age and, like her, a struggling musician. They kept their relationship quiet and assumed no one in the studio knew. But once Fusari found out what was going on, Kafafian, says the friend, was fired. Stefani couldn't figure out why, and she was crushed when Kafafian dumped her shortly after.

"She came to me so upset about it, very distraught," says the friend. "She was like, 'I'm so hurt.' I don't think she realized what was happening at the time." (Kafafian refuses to discuss the circumstances of his leaving and his breakup with Stefani or what role Fusari may have played in that.)

Stefani soon figured it out. Fusari, who, at thirty-six, was eighteen years Stefani's senior, made his feelings known. That he had a live-in fiancée named Jane—who would often drive Stefani to and from the bus stop in Jersey—did not seem to concern him. (Complicating matters further: Fusari's brother was married to Jane's sister.)

Stefani was overwhelmed: She didn't have strong feelings for him, if any. She wasn't so much worried about what would happen if she got involved with him—she was worried what would happen if she didn't.

"Basically, she really wanted [to make] her record," the friend says. In much the same way that, at first, "she wasn't even into this style of music, dance—it was not what came from her heart—she was like, 'OK, I'll try it out. And after trying it out for a while, she got the hang of it. I think she approached the relationship with Rob in a similar way: 'I may have signed up for a Tom, but . . .'" The friend pauses. "She really wanted to become famous and successful, and she worked really hard. And she was worried that if she didn't go through with it . . ."

So she went through with it.

It was a rough time. Her high school friends didn't like what she was doing with Fusari; they made it clear that they judged her for it, and their judgment wounded her. She was still upset about Kafafian, who says he had no idea what was going on. It's a plausible claim, given his propensity for statements such as "It's just about relishing the love. . . . I'm here because I'm here. Because there's no place you're not supposed to be."

Anyway: Kafafian says that, in his recollection, he left to go on tour with "this band" for three months, but that every time he tried to come back, or talk to Stefani or Fusari on the phone, he couldn't get through. He felt like he was getting frozen out. "They kind of forgot about me," he says, "even though I was trying to better myself."

Unlike Fusari, who later filed a $30.5 million lawsuit against Gaga that claimed she was attempting to cheat him out of monies owed, Kafafian says he's never considered going after payment for his work on tracks—including, he says, writing guitar parts and lyrics—that wound up on *The Fame*.

"I played my ass off on 'Beautiful, Dirty, Rich' and 'Brown Eyes,'" he says today. He finds the theme of *The Fame* highly ironic, given how used and left behind he feels. "Perhaps I was naïve," he says. "Sometimes you have to go through the craps to see the traps, as they say. Right now I know what I want, and I don't have to cut anyone down to get there. I don't really care. In my heart, I know what the truth is. But shame on them."

Stefani, meanwhile, was booking herself gigs wherever she could, sometimes as a dancer, sometimes as a musician, calling up clubs like the Bitter End—where she'd performed as an NYU student with the Stefani Germanotta Band—pretending to be her own publicist, talking up this new girl. That the guys who owned the Bitter End knew her from her days performing with the Stefani Germanotta Band didn't stop her. "The venue guys watched me grow up musically in the clubs," she said.

She booked herself into Arlene's Grocery, a small club on Stanton Street that was just a few doors down from the Slipper Room. Like most of the venues on the Lower East Side, Arlene's primarily booked rock acts. "But we booked her because she said she could bring fifty people to the show," says Julia Dee, who was the club's booker back then. "And she did."

The scenesters who worked at Arlene's were typically underwhelmed, as per the neighborhood's code of conduct. "I remember the staff members were [like], 'Hot body, can't sing,'" Dee says. "She was in bikini bottoms, playing the keyboard. We thought that was pretty out there." Dee dropped her after a second booking drew only eight people. "The music was cheesy, dated pop with an R&B feel to it," she says, the "same kind of stuff she's doing now." This sentiment is typical of the Lower East Side's too-cool-for-school circular logic: Back then, Lady Gaga wasn't cool enough to play in a venue that hosted unknowns night after night after night, and now that she's become a critically acclaimed international pop star, they still think she's not good enough.

Everyone at the Bitter End, however, thought she was gifted: "It was an easy booking," says Bitter End co-owner Paul Rizzo. "She is an incredible talent." That didn't mean they thought she would make it: "There is a lot more involved than talent," says Rizzo. "And she was good, but I see so many people come through that don't go anywhere. The ones that do—it's very hard to figure out. There's no formula to it."

Rizzo says that Stefani played her first gig at the Bitter End as Gaga on July 28, 2006. He still has a poster downstairs from that gig, he says: Gaga in green hot pants, arms thrown back— "disco ball included," he adds dryly. And no Gaga anecdote would be complete without an accounting of what she was wearing that night—it struck him, he says, because it was so different from her earlier days: "She was just a little more . . . in a different-type outfit," he says diplomatically. "I think she was wearing, like, a yellow-and-black one-piece. And some sort of hat."

Gaga recalled the Bitter End as her first real show, but recalled the outfit a bit differently: She was in an American Apparel one-piece, she said. "I had a white skirt on, giant white, with a fucking flower in my hair. I looked like such a loser. I had an Amy Winehouse beehive—before she came out."

If there's one thing Gaga can't stand, it's the idea that she's aggressively copied someone else's look. Because she so obviously, inarguably *has,* her outrage is almost funny. Just a year later at Lollapalooza, where she'd been booked for one of the lesser stages, she found herself hounded by paparazzi as well as regular people who wanted her picture. They thought she was Amy Winehouse. It was, at the very least, a fortuitous bit of confusion. She didn't like it, but she played along, telling a fan who'd mistaken her for Winehouse to "fuck off!" The girl scooted away, thrilled that her idol had just cursed her.

Her songwriting was going well. Surprisingly, says Starland, her relationship with Fusari deepened. She found herself involved, even though she'd embarked on the relationship not even halfheartedly—quarter-heartedly?—and even though Fusari still had a fiancée. Starland recalls asking him why he would jeopardize his current relationship; he told her that the prospect of the money and the fame "was a rush." Both, she says, were addicted to the melodrama that was their relationship, what each could do for the other.

Fusari was also inspiring some of her writing, including the aforementioned "Brown Eyes," a song that, in concert, she now often ends by raging at the song's subject, calling him "motherfucker!!!!" and mocking "your bullshit brown eyes."

"I was dating somebody that I couldn't be with," Gaga has said. "I wrote that at three A.M., crying in front of the piano. Wailing in front of a Yamaha."

"Blueberry Kisses," Starland says, is also about Rob: "They used to have blueberry pancakes in the morning," she says. "They had a serious connection." They also had very similar personalities: volatile, dramatic, contentious. "The highs were really high, and the lows were really low," says Starland. "They were both going crazy." At one of the lowest points in her relationship with Fusari, Gaga called her mother to come out to New Jersey for moral support.

At her most tired and tormented, she doubted whether she

had the fortitude or the ability to see the demo through. "She'd say, 'I don't know if I can finish this record,'" says Starland.

And what would Starland tell her friend? "You're a professional. I didn't fucking spend all this time and energy and work writing these songs and creating a vision with you, putting all this together, dealing with every facet of drama for you to say, 'I don't know if I can deal with it.'"

Meanwhile, Stefani was still struggling to break into the upper echelons of the Lower East Side scene. She'd been dancing with Starlight at St. Jerome's and had gotten herself booked at the Slipper Room, but, ever the overachiever, she wanted promoters Michael T. and Justine D.—two of downtown's biggest stars, who conceived of and threw parties on their own and for clubs and other clients—to hire her for their Motherfucker events.

A series of roaming, dissolute, debauched parties held on the nights before major holidays, Motherfucker events—not unlike the DJ collective and weekly party known as MisShapes—dominated downtown nightlife from 2003 to 2008, eventually attracting thousands of partygoers, among them the "bridge-and-tunnelers" who commuted from suburban Long Island or New Jersey. (Bridge-and-tunnelers, who are usually identified by their suburban styling and overreliance on hair product, are considered complete undesirables among the city's self-styled fabulous, who themselves often come from suburban Long Island or New Jersey.)

The Motherfucker parties would traditionally close with

Diana Ross's 1976 disco hit "Love Hangover," in tribute to Studio 54, and access was granted by one of the scene's toughest, most infamous doormen, Thomas Onorato. As Glenn Belverio, author of *Confessions from the Velvet Ropes,* put it in a 2006 blog post: "Remember: Motherfucker is a dictatorship at the door and a democracy on the dance floor—so work a look or New York's #1 doorman, Thomas Onorato, will send you straight to the New Year's gulag." But Motherfucker wasn't really a dictatorship—all you had to do was pay to get in. The threat of rejection, though, is always a great selling point.

Lady Starlight, it turned out, knew Michael T., who knew her by her real name, Colleen Martin. At the time, Martin was working as a makeup artist at a M.A.C store by day and, in addition to her own gigs, had often been hired to dance by Michael T. for Motherfucker and another party he did called Rated X. Martin began bringing Gaga around to Motherfucker bashes in 2007.

"Certainly her look was completely eighties stripper rock trash," says Michael T. "She looked like something out of 1987." He was perplexed by just what bonded the two girls, but noted that Martin's younger friend was unabashedly aping her look.

"Colleen, at that point, was also looking really heavy-metal trashy," he says. "She had a grown-out shag—dark on top and literally fried blond at the tips. She did it on purpose; it was definitely funny." Stefani's look, by contrast, seemed earnest; she appeared to have put herself together that way because she genuinely thought it looked good. She'd not yet picked up that esoteric trick of telegraphing irony and wit through carefully cultivated bad taste.

To Michael T., it seemed that Gaga had no personal, cohesive style: "I mean, I suppose, like anybody, she was probably taking a lot of what she was seeing from her friends," he says. "But I can tell you that between Colleen's Bowie impression and Lady Gaga's—night and day. Colleen looked like a freak from 1973. Gaga looked like somebody had said, 'Oh, let's put a David Bowie lightning bolt on your face.'"

Gaga wanted Michael T. to hire her to dance at his parties. She auditioned. "She was OK," he says, laughing. "I wasn't floored." But he was friendly with Lüc the bartender, who Michael T. recalls as Gaga's boyfriend by this time. (She was still involved with Fusari, but Lüc, by all accounts, had no idea they had anything other than a professional relationship.)

"Colleen would tell me she was doing this act with her," Michael T. says, "but just the way it was being described, I really did not take it seriously. Like, really? Like, live DJ, two dancers, and Lady Gaga looking like a heavy-metal queen?" The Gaga moniker barely registered with him, harking back as it did to the nineties club scene, when twenty-nine-year-old "club kids" ran around town with names like "Pebbles" and "Desi Monster."

Michael T. relented, hiring Gaga—with Lüc—to host a Motherfucker party DJ'd by Moby at the now-defunct, superplush club Eugene on 24th Street between Fifth and Sixth avenues.

The job description, according to him: "Look good, invite cute friends and bands, drink, work for about three hours."

She didn't make much of an impression on doorman Thomas Onorato. "She was friends with my friend Lüc, who was also a host that night," he says. "She was one of eight to ten promo-sexual hosts—that's what we called them. She was brunette at that point. That's really all I can tell you."

"I remember she looked nice," says Michael T. "Sort of like the heavy-metal stripper girl going for a fancy night out. She wore a long gown, I want to say maybe pink or salmon, with a low-cut back."

Even though Gaga didn't seem *of* the downtown rock scene, Michael T. understood why she wanted to be in it. "Suddenly, something happened" in New York, he says. "Electroclash had been over and done with for a number of years." But it would hugely inform Gaga's music. Cult electroclash artists such as Felix Da Housecat and Miss Kittin ironically wrote about fame and paparazzi culture, playing with the idea of being superstars in a scene that would abide no such thing. Gaga was also influenced by their fuzzy, filthy syncopated beats, but she would clean them up, make them less challenging and more radio-friendly.

Dance parties were replacing rock shows. Kids were gravitating toward stuff that felt under-the-radar, dirty, secret, elitist, and judgmental—even though, ostensibly, the downtown scene was about welcoming all freaks and misfits. It wasn't, and never really has been; you had to be the right kind of misfit—cool, or cool enough. Or, in Gaga's case, friends with people who were cool and would help you out, vouch for you, let you be their "+1," in nightlife parlance.

But everything was, and is, degrees, as it always has been in New York City. On the Lower East Side, knowing where the newest secret bar was located was good; having the number was better; knowing the owner and having unlimited access was enough to validate one's self-worth for a good few weeks, till everyone figured it out and something else as supposedly secret and stupidly exclusive sprang up to replace it.

Similarly, it wasn't enough to just know about a secret rock show; you had to be on the list, know about not the official after-party but the *after*-after party, post pictures of you with the band to LastNightsParty. This was the era when actual superstars, high-profile *Vogue* magazine editors, and pristine uptown socialites began actively courting and taking cues from the kids behind the Motherfucker and MisShapes dance parties, and the cool kids, operating as rejects from the mainstream, were suddenly the gate-keepers.

MisShapes was a weekly, Sunday-night gathering of hipsters celebrating themselves and their general level of street cred, DJ'd and overseen by suburban transplants Geordon Nicol, Leigh Lezark, and Greg Krelenstein. MisShapes was for the very young; if you were twenty-six you could easily feel like you'd aged out. Unlike the electroclash scene and Motherfucker parties, MisShapes was exclusive; it was very much about who you knew and what you looked like, and it was most definitely not open to all. It was their playlist that was the most radical thing about the parties: They embraced mainstream pop music, playing artists, such as Madonna, who would never be heard at a cool-kids gathering downtown unless it was done with the explicit understanding that this was mocking.

The apotheosis of this came when Madonna asked if she could DJ (for a few minutes) at a MisShapes party in October 2005. The MisShapes went on to do national print ads for Eastport backpacks, and Lezark is now a front-row presence at New York and Paris fashion weeks—such is the wide-ranging currency of downtown New York cool in the early twenty-first century. These were the people Gaga wanted to get next to, impress, study. She may not have had good taste herself, but she knew who did and was determined to get it for herself.

"She was definitely in the scene," says Michael T., "and making those rounds."

During this time, Gaga had two confidantes. Lady Starlight was one. Wendy Starland was the other. Both were older than she was, both were in a position to assist her professionally, but neither ever felt exploited. They wanted to help, and they liked hanging out with her. She was fun and sweet, generous and generally bubbly, but unafraid to be vulnerable and needy when it came to her anxiety over boys and her career. She did love to talk about herself to the exclusion of most everything else.

"We would go out all the time," Starland says. "We'd go out to bars, to concerts. We went to see the Philharmonic. We spoke on the phone, like, three times a day. I'm spending Christmas with her family. She'd sleep at my house, come to me for advice on her personal affairs." Starland says Gaga had difficulty being alone, hated it, that when she slept over she couldn't even stay on the couch—that was too solitary. She'd crawl into bed with Starland, who says it was just for company, nothing more. "She was a night owl, but Rob had gotten her into being an early riser." Often, Gaga would stop by Wendy's in the morning, coffee and brown-bagged take-out breakfast in hand.

Fusari, however, didn't fully approve of the friendship: "He didn't like it when the two of us would go out," says Starland. "He feared we'd get a lot of attention from boys or whatever." Still, he'd also ask Starland for advice about his relationship with Gaga.

Whether out of perversion, revenge, or cowardice, sometimes Rob would bring Jane to meet the girls for dinner. "Tension started brewing around that time," Starland says. "I think Jane started to suspect, and I think she started checking his phone for texts."

Gaga would also check Fusari's phone for texts from Jane— if he stepped out of the studio for a moment, she'd scurry over and scroll through his log, and if she found a message from Jane, she'd blow up. Then she'd eventually calm down and real-ize the absurdity of the situation and apologize to Fusari.

Another friend of Gaga's from this time period is loath to talk about Fusari: "It honestly doesn't matter what I tell you about what happened with her and Rob, [because] it's gonna look bad," she says. "But she didn't do anything wrong."

At the same time, Fusari and Starland wanted Laurent Besencon, who managed Fusari, to take on Gaga as a client. He said no. Her look was a problem. She and Fusari pressed on. They posted finished versions of "Paparazzi" and "Beautiful, Dirty, Rich" on MySpace. Gaga also did a "media buy"—basically, she bought space to be featured prominently for a couple of weeks—at PureVolume.com. It was an interesting choice; the site is mainly devoted to emo, which, without diminishing it, is a genre mainly devoted to lodging complaints: at the world, at one's parents, at romantic interests that are largely unrequited, at one's friends, at oneself. Gaga's Euro-inflected, get-fucked-up-and-dance aesthetic was at utter odds with the site's: It was the prom queen playing Dungeons & Dragons on a Friday night in some geek's moldy suburban basement, or the social outcast daring to sit with the cool kids in the back of the bus, depending on your worldview.

"I was very confused as to why she would be doing such a huge push on PureVolume," says Sarah Lewitinn, who, at the time, worked in A&R at Island/Def Jam. "I thought she had a good voice, but it was hard to tell what was going on. I couldn't tell if she was trying to go for a Michelle Branch, Paramore angle or what. She had a very different look to her than anything you would see on PureVolume. It didn't really show any of the David-Bowie-meets-Madonna-meets-Britney-Spears angles that she eventually transformed into."

Gaga was still trying to decode her own artistic DNA: She knew that she—like all musical acts—needed a look that was a distinct image that would become a marketable, readily identifiable brand. But she had no idea what it should be.

For all her later talk about being an artsy misfit outsider, she was really just a nice Catholic girl from the Upper West Side who was never a big reader, who shopped at expensive, generically tasteful boutiques like Olive and Bette's, who just wanted everyone to like her.

"I was the girl," she told her label's biographer, "with [Britney's] name written all over my face, crying at *TRL* because I saw her hand." Her vocal coach, at sixteen, was Don Lawrence, who'd also worked with Mick Jagger, Bono, and Christina

Aguilera. "Gaga's parents always had her connected with the best people," says Sullivan. "She worked with [Don] always." To this day, she travels with a recording of Lawrence's vocal exercises.

Lawrence introduced the young Stefani to execs at the Disney Channel and suggested she audition to replace the lead singer of a sugary teen girl group called No Secrets, who appear on their album cover in matching white jeans and unfortunate two-tone hoodies. They got their start in 2001, in the Fordlândia teenage factory that produced the 'N Sync/Britney/Christina Aguilera/Backstreet Boys teen-pop explosion of the nineties, first singing backup for Backstreet Boy Nick Carter's scrawny, abrasive little brother, Aaron, on the unfortunately titled songs "Oh Aaron" and "Stride (Jump on the Fizzy)."

"It gave me a taste of the record industry," Gaga said of making the teen-pop-factory rounds. "I thought I was about to become Whitney Houston. But you don't realize what that takes until later."

While shopping around for a record deal, Gaga continued booking as many live shows as she could, now sometimes performing as the Plastic Gaga Band. "I played in every club in New York City," she said. "I bombed in every club, and then I killed it in every club. I did it the way you are supposed to: You go and you play and pay your dues and work hard." Around this time, Besencon was convinced to see her live; he did, and he finally signed on to manage her.

The viral success of the two singles she'd posted online

became her leverage with record labels; she was a best seller in cyberspace, so why *wouldn't* they take a meeting with her?

"She is perfectly, almost genetically engineered to be a twenty-first-century pop star," says Eric Garland. As CEO of BigChampagne.com, Garland is an expert in the consumption of music online; his company tracks data, including peer-to-peer file sharing, for all the major labels.

Gaga, he says, "is an incredibly social animal in the new definition of social. She's sort of promiscuous. And I don't mean promiscuous in the Ke$ha sense—I mean socially promiscuous online." (Ke$ha is the pop singer who styles herself as the avant-gardist of the trailer park, who does what she can to draw comparisons to Gaga.) But it was Gaga's innate understanding of creating and cultivating an online identity—and a sense of community with those who responded—that would, as much as major-label backing, catapult her into global consciousness. She would later actively cultivate the support of gossip blogger Perez Hilton, whose site, as of April 2010, was ranked 192 in most-trafficked websites in the United States and 517th globally.

As for the brick-and-mortar music business, the earthbound major labels: Gaga got a lot of no's. They would say she didn't have the right look, that they didn't hear any hits in the material. She didn't stop trying. She tried to get a publishing deal—basically, a contract to write songs that could be sold to other artists—with Irwin Robinson, her old boss at Famous Music. He said no. She tried to get a publishing deal with Sony/ATV; they said no. Her meeting at Sony/ATV, according to a source, was with Danny Goldberg, who had managed Nirvana and had run three major labels. She was there with Fusari, which should have conferred a level of respect, but Gaga felt Goldberg wasn't listening to a thing she was saying, that he couldn't have made his disinterest clearer. She left the meeting in a rage, yelling at Fusari that she would never sign to Sony/ATV. Then she took her act up to the Island Def Jam offices in midtown Manhattan to audition for a deal in late 2006.

An Island Def Jam employee remembers seeing Gaga coming down the hall: "She reminded me of Julia Roberts [in] *Pretty Woman*," she says. "But in American Apparel."

What happened that afternoon at Island Def Jam has become part of the Gaga myth, and even one of her closest friends from this time—who was not present but heard about the audition from Gaga immediately afterward—tells it the same way: Gaga sang and played piano for a gaggle of execs. She saw one, out of the corner of her eye, get up and leave; she panicked, but you'd never have been able to tell by looking at her. She kept going and, when she was done, looked up to see label head Antonio "L.A." Reid in the doorway. He said, "See legal on your way out"—industry-speak for "We're signing you."

It didn't really go down that way, according to someone who was in the room. For one thing, her appointment that day was with Reid himself: "She walked into L.A.'s office," says the source. "A couple of minutes later, someone asked me if I would go watch Gaga do a showcase *in* L.A.'s office."

Also in the room: Gaga's future artist and repertoire person Josh Sarubin; senior VP Karen Kwak, also known as Reid's right-hand woman; and a few others. Reid had a tiny room off his office, maybe ten feet by ten feet, outfitted with an upright piano; this is where Gaga auditioned.

"She sat down at the piano and introduced herself," says the source. "Then she started playing—she did 'Beautiful, Dirty, Rich' and a few other songs. She was amazing. There was no doubt about it—the minute you saw her behind her instrument, you knew she was special. But the thing is—and I know I'm not the only person who thinks this—I don't remember anything about the songs, because the whole time we could not take our eyes off her ass. She was in this tight little skirt or tube dress. She moved back and forth and you could just see her ass cheeks running up and down, like on a seesaw almost. Everyone was looking around the room with these giant smiles, looking at her ass."

After her mini-set, she turned around to face Reid, and this part of the story actually aligns with the myth. Says the source: "L.A. just goes, 'I want you to march downstairs to Business Affairs and we're going to offer you a deal. Don't leave the building till you sign.'"

Gaga met with the label's lawyer, and when she got hold of her own attorney, he asked her who over at the label was handling the deal. Her lawyer told her that the Island Def Jam deal was going to be big—the label had tasked one of their best lawyers with handling it.

"She would say, 'I'll be with this lawyer for the rest of my life; that will never change,'" says Starland. "Her lawyer is no longer her lawyer anymore. That will be a common theme."

♦ ♦ ♦

Her contract, according to Gaga, was huge: She told friends
that Island Def Jam signed her to an $850,000 deal. Jim Gueri-
not, who manages, among others, Nine Inch Nails, No Doubt,
and the Offspring, says there's no way Gaga signed a deal worth
anything near $850,000.

"I don't believe it," he says. "That's how ridiculous it is. To
give an unknown that much money and a distribution deal . . .
Huh? Highly successful artists can occasionally get deals of
that nature. It's absolutely unheard of for new artists."

One person who was in the room for the signing and saw
the contract insists that $850,000 was the exact figure, and it
was Fusari's very recent, very huge successes with Destiny's
Child and Jessica Simpson that secured Gaga such a huge deal.
But another industry veteran says he, too, finds this deal highly,
highly unlikely.

"Rarely in the last ten years were artists getting a check for
anything north of $500,000," he says. "It's so hard to believe
that one artist is getting $850,000 for one album. I don't know
the terms—there are so many factors. It could've been a five-
album deal." Fusari's involvement might have been a help, he
says, but even the producer's reputation would not have trans-
lated into that much money. "But you know," he adds, "I've seen
crazy shit. There are some bulldog New York attorneys who
may get that money."

Whatever money she was making had to be divided up. She,
Joe, and Fusari had formed a production company together,

and it was the company, not Gaga, that was technically signed to Island Def Jam.

In addition to her 80-20 deal with Fusari, her new manager Besencon was getting a 20 percent cut of everything. Starland, who'd discovered Gaga and was cowriting songs with her, had only a verbal agreement that she, too, would get a cut of any future deal, and she was not pleased when Gaga offered to give her just publishing rights; Starland would only be able to collect if anything she wrote wound up on the record. Starland says Gaga also offered to pay her a $10,000 flat fee.

"I was like, 'That's nice, but given that Laurent's been in the picture a very, very short time and I've been doing this development, I feel I deserve at least half of what Laurent makes—10 percent, and some publishing on two of the songs,'" Starland recalls. "And she was like, 'That's totally fair.'"

A few days later, Starland says she sat down with Gaga and Fusari at a restaurant on the Upper West Side to go over the terms of the deal. "He said, 'Wendy, we will all work out something fair and equitable—this would not be happening without you,'" she says. "And I was like, 'Great, so can my lawyer be in touch?' and he said, 'Absolutely.'"

Now that she had a deal, Gaga had to hone her stagecraft and her image as fast as possible. She couldn't afford a stylist and didn't really have an eye, so she was still relying on the hipster porno-chic of American Apparel. But it only made her appear overtly, plainly sexual, not edgy or outré.

So she started to experiment with stage looks, which mainly meant performing in her bra or a bikini top. She was young still, only twenty-one years old, and had not been properly introduced to the figures, mainstream and cult, she would later so successfully reappropriate. Gaga, though, has engaged in a bit of revisionist history, talking about her "underground New York following."

"The shows, at that time, were shock art," she said. "I was like the Damien Hirst of pop music, doing something so offensive. In that neighborhood, it's junkies and metalheads—how do I get them to come and listen to pop music? I take my clothes off, I use a lot of hairspray, and I write songs about oral sex." It should be noted that in downtown New York City, in 2007, absolutely none of that behavior would have been considered shocking. Quaint, maybe. Or a nice try.

Around this time, Gaga befriended a girl her age who doesn't want to be identified; she worked for a small music publishing company and spent about six or seven months hanging out with Gaga constantly. "One night," says the friend, "she was doing this show at the Bitter End, and she wanted to find a shirt and she literally took the subway to Queens for it. It was funny—she was wearing one of those wife-beater [tank tops], but as a dress. But it wasn't American Apparel—it was, like, Hanes. And she ended up finding this piece of jewelry she was looking for. We were like, 'Stefani, what are you doing?' She almost missed the show. We were like, 'This chick will go out to Queens to pick up a piece of jewelry.' Everything about her was crazy and original."

FOUR

ART OF THE STEAL

*G*aga kept calling around town on her own behalf, trying to book herself into clubs and parties. Her success, as ever, was scattershot. "I remember she used to call around and ask people, because she did call us," says New York City nightlife fixture Ladyfag, who at the time was, along with well-known club kid Kenny Kenny, behind a party called Sebastian. She has trouble recalling exactly when this was, but she says Gaga's performances had been generating buzz, so she booked her.

"It was her and two other girls," says Ladyfag, "and she was wearing a bra and high-waisted panties with mirrors all over them. And it was just a big joke. Everyone was kind of making fun: 'Who does she think she is, coming in here?'"

That said, Ladyfag thought Gaga was great. "She did maybe three or four songs, and one of them was 'Boys Boys Boys.' She was fabulous. It was a great performance." Contrary to her backstory, Ladyfag says Gaga was not a presence in gay clubs, either as a performer or a partier. (In New York City, gay clubs have long been places where trends and careers are launched.) Actively cultivating a gay following, as a performer, says two things: You are open-minded and nondiscriminatory, and you know that a gay fan base not only tends to be incredibly loyal but quite often ahead of the mainstream curve.

"I have nothing bad to say about her, but she is trying to create this whole myth," says Ladyfag. "It's not like she was some kid who ran away from home and was hanging out in all the gay clubs, 'cause that's so not true." She laughs. "It's not true. She played a few gay parties, but that was after her album came out. Before she became really big."

It's hard to say how much the creation myth accounts for Gaga's meteoric, global rise. But it's clear that her music, so polished and accessible, is in no way avant-garde. As talented as she is, she never would have broken through without the wackiness. "Most likely it wasn't the music, an electro-soul mélange that has made Lady Gaga famous despite its contentedly low aims," wrote the *New York Times*'s Jon Caramanica in a review of her first big NYC gig, at Midtown venue Terminal 5, six months after *The Fame* had been released. He went on to call her music "an odorless, colorless, almost unnecessary additive to the Lady Gaga spectacle."

In a review of *The Fame* in the UK's *Guardian* newspaper, critic Alexis Petridis pilloried her for her claims of fantastical uniqueness, both musically and aesthetically. Her success, he wrote in his January 2009 piece, "seems to have led Lady Gaga to come to some pretty bullish conclusions about her own originality: 'I'm defying all the preconceptions we have of pop artists,' she recently told one journalist, seemingly confident of a place in the history books as the world's first pretty female singer performing synthesizer-heavy R&B-influenced pop. 'I'm very into fashion,' she clarified, all previous pretty female singers having apparently performed their synthesizer-heavy R&B-influenced pop clad in stuff they grabbed at random from the George at Asda half-price sale."

And yet, in an age of confessional culture, in which "reality" is routinely put on display in tabloids, on TV, on the Web, and we regularly see, as she put it, "legends taking out the trash," Lady Gaga managed to explode on the pop-music scene as a fully formed entity. Aside from those few performance clips on the Web, there was no trace of the "guidette" Fusari met, very little documentation of Gaga's development.

Actually, given the ready-made nature of her sound, it's even more incredible that Gaga sold by-the-numbers dance tracks as mini-revolutions of the soul and a major revolution in the direction of pop music. It's a true feat of performance art.

"She did a brilliant job of reinventing herself as a naked, visual spectacle that was backed up by really solid songwriting," says Tony DiSanto, president of programming and development at MTV. He is sitting with Liz Gateley, the network's VP of series development and the mastermind behind *The Hills,* in his office in Times Square. The space, like DiSanto himself, is welcoming and unpretentious: There are a few framed pictures and gold records, but these sit low on the windowsill; the medium-sized office is dominated by a huge flat-screen TV, which is situated between a black leather sofa and DiSanto's desk. He is in blue jeans and a black shirt, ankle across his knee.

"When I started hearing the buzz, it was through people who were tweeting through Facebook. I'll never forget her first big show here in New York"—on May 2, 2009, the Terminal 5 show. DiSanto—who is in his forties, yet whose shock of black hair and natural exuberance makes him seem much younger—wasn't there, but he remembers getting "an explosion" of texts and tweets from people in the industry who were.

"It reminded me of when Guns 'N Roses did that show at the Ritz in 1988"—which was an MTV special taped in New York—"and all of a sudden it was like we'd just seen the second coming of rock. Her buzz explosion through social media was, for me, this generation's version of the Guns 'N Roses Ritz show."

There are only two other performers in recent memory who exploded globally via the Internet: Susan Boyle, the sensitive recluse exploited to brilliant effect by Simon Cowell & Co., and Justin Bieber, the teenage Canadian with an asymmetrical helmet of chestnut hair and dead eyes. Gaga, however, "created a buzz factor for herself before we ever saw an image of her," says Liz Gateley. Gateley, like DiSanto, is in her forties, yet she, too, with her expensive blond hair, slim frame, and warm manner, comes across as an eternal teenager.

"A year and a half ago," she continues, "my head of talent came to me and said, 'You have to do something with this person.' The buzz was so big, but her imagery had not reached the mainstream fifteen-year-old girl in Iowa yet." Gateley and DiSanto say they knew it wasn't a matter of if Gaga was going to break, but when; they began a series of talks with her people about doing a documentary that would use, fittingly, *Madonna:*

Truth or Dare as a template. And then, says Gateley, she just "fired off"—went from no one knowing who she was to mainstream fame so fast that the network lost its window. "We couldn't even get a time to sit down with her and talk about it," Gateley says.

Gaga came across, immediately, as both a total original and a walking, derivative mash-up of the greatest pop androgynes of the twentieth century: the aforementioned Bowie, Madonna, Prince. For the urban sophisticate who consumes pop culture, there are deeper, more rewarding references, rivulets leading to tributaries: There's the late visionary artist, promoter, and dandy Leigh Bowery and singer and performance artist Klaus Nomi, provocateurs and source material for the likes of Boy George (Bowery) and David Bowie (Nomi).

Bowery especially—with his Kabuki-white face, super-exaggerated black lips, and plump body aggressively distorted by painful clothes—made it purposefully difficult to look at him. At times, he didn't even seem human; as Bowery and Nomi had before, Gaga can make it hard to look at her. She spent the first year of her celebrity wrapping up her face, and still sometimes does; it can be such a visual assault that you have to strain to work through whatever thicket is obscuring her head. At the 2009 MTV Video Music Awards, for example, she wore a red lace minidress, the material snaked up and around her neck and face like some out-of-control haute-couture network of vines—a direct reference to the same look in the late designer Alexander McQueen's 1998–1999 fall/winter show. (McQueen wound up dressing her and giving her access to his archives, and she wore a head-to-toe look from one of his last collections, made famous for its outsized, sequined "armadillo" shoes, in the "Bad Romance" video.)

Gaga would borrow something deeper from both Bowery and Nomi: the tragic image of the artist as married to the art, forever a loser in love, intermittently sated by random sex but relying on the adulation of the audience to live, devoted to them above all. She currently claims to be single and celibate, but as of this writing, she is actually involved with her stylist, Matt Williams, and has been for some time. "When you're lonely," she says to her audience in the short film that runs at the end of her current show, her face repeatedly contorted and distorted, "I'll be lonely, too." It's a poignant message in this age of false intimacy, of five hundred Facebook friends one never actually sees and thousands of Twitter followers one's never met.

The current list of Gaga influences is vast and interdisciplinary, and though she claims they're all personal favorites, those who know her well say they've never really heard her discuss the more esoteric ones. The people and things she's always cited, they say, are hardly obscure: Andy Warhol, Chanel, Donatella Versace. In much the same way her high school and college friends attest that she was a normal, well-adjusted teenager with mainstream interests, those who'd later ask Gaga about her avant-garde reference points would find themselves talking to a flummoxed girl.

"She'd been talking about Warhol and Bowie and Grace Jones—those were her talking points," says journalist Jonah Weiner, who interviewed Lady Gaga for a *Blender* magazine cover story in late February 2009 (it never ran; the magazine folded). He says, though, that when he'd ask her a follow-up question, "You'd see she didn't have an answer prepared, and she'd get cagier. You could see her discomfort level rise. I'd ask her about Warhol and she'd say, 'He believed that pop culture could be high art, and I believe the same thing.' And if I asked her to [expound], she couldn't do it."

When she brought up the controversial 1974 film *The Night Porter,* starring Charlotte Rampling as a concentration camp survivor who embarks upon a sadomasochistic affair with the Nazi who tortured her—fashion people love this movie, maybe because it's so transgressive, but probably for the scene in which Rampling wears tailored pants with suspenders and no shirt and looks utterly chic—Weiner says Gaga was out of her depth. He asked her about the film's theme, about the notion, he says, "of the victim falling in love with the tormenter. [For her], it was more about how sexy Charlotte Rampling was." (One question Weiner, who found himself liking her despite having a low opinion of her music, regrets omitting: "I don't know why I didn't ask her why she was into this *Eurotrash house,*" he says, laughing.)

It's in this way, too, that Lady Gaga is so obviously a product of the Internet age. No longer does familiarizing oneself with the obscure require tenacity and legwork and fruitless trips to vintage vinyl or magazine shops (which hardly exist anymore). Now you just Google it or Wiki it or download it to your iPod and go down the electronic rabbit hole of references—and that's not a bad thing. But it does tend to result in a facile working knowledge of once-obscure people and art and movements, and that kind of surface knowledge, when masquerading as deep immersion, can be an affront. An underprepared Lady Gaga claiming a deep affinity with decades-old countercultural figures does not go down well with music journalists, critics, and obsessives, whose outsider interests tend to reflect inner alienaton.

She was not as knowledgable as you'd expect during a 2009 interview on the Fuse music network; when the journalist Touré asked, "Do you know what 'Strong J' means?" Gaga was taken aback. "Strong J?" she asked. "I'm talking about Grace Jones," Touré said, and Gaga quickly recovered: "Yeah, yeah, Grace is a huge inspiration to me." Jones is not impressed: "Well, you know, I've seen some things she's worn that I've worn," she recently told the *Guardian,* "and that does kind of piss me off." (Jones's second album, by the way, was called *Fame.*)

From German singer Nina Hagen and Missing Persons' Dale Bozzio, Gaga stole a rough, aggressive sexuality that never read as actually sexy. (There are pictures of Bozzio that, placed side by side with Lady Gaga, look indistinguishable.) From early Peter Gabriel, Leigh Bowery, and Boy George she stole the Kabuki-like face paint. From Icelandic pop star Björk—who lives with art star Matthew Barney, and who had a then unknown McQueen design her 1997 album cover for *Homogenic*—she stole the aesthetic futurism and the impression that she, too, routinely receives transmissions from another planet. (Back in 1995, when Björk was reaching the heights of her creativity, Madonna stole directly from *her*—the kimonos, the space-age techno beats—filming a hallucinatory video for "Bedtime Story," a single that Madonna commissioned from Björk, who, according to industry legend, at first wrote lyrics criticizing Madonna's unoriginality.)

Moving on: From Marilyn Manson and Alice Cooper, Gaga stole the scary makeup, the androgyny, and the construct that she is Lady Gaga 24/7, that this alter-ego long ago subsumed her former identity, that she is never off-duty. (The latter notion is also borrowed from Prince.) She borrowed Gwen Stefani's sound, and has cited her as a huge inspiration: "[Gwen]'s lined her lips with red since we saw her and she's never stopped," Gaga said. "It's so powerful to me. Her fame was in her mouth. I don't know where mine is yet . . . my vagina or my hair."

From Liza Minnelli and Judy Garland, she's stolen a propensity for overwrought ballads and the tragedy of the overly made-up, romantically unfulfilled chanteuse loved primarily by gay men. From Bette Midler, she stole the outrageous stagecraft and costumes, the unspoken triumph of the unconventional-looking underdog-cum-diva who'd be nowhere without the gays. From the late British fashion muse Isabella Blow—who discovered McQueen—she has stolen many indelible looks almost wholesale. Gaga, as it turns out, was not the first woman to wear a lobster hat. Blow was. (McQueen and Blow were likely inspired by the 1937 collaboration between Elsa Schiaparelli and Salvador Dalí that resulted in their famed Lobster Dress.)

It's unclear who turned her on to the likes of Bowery and Nomi, obscure pop culture figures who never attained the fame they so desired, but whose art, aesthetics, and attitudes were ripped off, to greater and greater effect, by successive generations. Nomi, who died of AIDS three years before Gaga was born, was a German ex-pat in New York, a trained opera singer who also covered pop songs. He'd perform at the Mudd Club, Max's Kansas City, and Danceteria, and worked the same kind of exaggerated silhouette—the aerodynamic shoulder pads that created the effect of an inverted triangle over the torso—that Lady Gaga would eventually adopt.

Weiner says that, during his interview with her for *Blender,* Nomi was one of her references, though she only spoke of him in generalities. She didn't give Nomi specific credit for her look: "She said, 'A lot of triangles pop up in my outfits,'" Weiner recalls. "'I like the phallic presentation.' She really enjoys talking about the semiotics of her outfits; she was very studious about how she dressed as this pop/sex symbol to be devoured. But she didn't want to go down smooth; she wanted to be pointy, to get stuck in your throat."

Another concept she took from Nomi: the presentation of the artist as a fake. In the 2005 documentary *The Nomi Song,* one admirer explained that Nomi's appeal had to do with "the cult of pure artifice and alienation in a culture that has become obsessed with authenticity."

Madonna, of course, mastered that years ago. And it's from Madonna that Gaga has stolen just about everything: the sexual and cultural provocations that made her generic pop music that much more interesting; the constant, very serious invocation of "my art"; the cultivation of the gay audience and vocal activism for their cause; the incessant reinvention and reincarnations. At the end of 1991's *Madonna: Truth or Dare,* she's onstage performing one of her more lackluster numbers—a bland track about family called "Keep It Together"—but she's throwing in anachronistic, countercultural references and self-help platitudes.

Both Madonna and Gaga source dialogue and costumes from the hyper-stylized film version of *A Clockwork Orange,* Stanley Kubrick's controversial take on violent, stylish youth run wild in London. In this performance, Madonna's wearing a black bowler hat identical to the one Malcolm McDowell wears in the movie, and quotes his character's euphemism for sex: "A little of the ol' 'in-out, in-out.'" Gaga played the famous score to the film before her show for two years, but claimed she stole that from Bowie, not Madonna.

Both enjoy dispensing motivational advice.

"Most importantly, never doubt yourselves," Madonna tells the crowd.

"You have to love yourself to succeed," Gaga told the crowd in April 2010, in Japan. "That's what I did."

"She took direction from Madonna," says MTV's Gateley, "but she's done it even more brilliantly. Madonna would change images every year, every two years. Lady Gaga changes her image every week."

One of the constant criticisms about Lady Gaga is that she is far too shrewd and calculating to be as crazy as she presents. "Gaga is not odd," wrote Sasha Frere-Jones in an April 27, 2009, piece in the *New Yorker.* He praised her talent and smarts and rightly predicted that *The Fame* would dominate 2009, but dismissed her invocation of influences like Communist red and Rilke as preposterous: "You can't find Marx or Rilke anywhere in the music," he wrote.

Frere-Jones had a point about the Communist red: It sounds cool, but it's not a motif in her work. He wasn't wrong about the Rilke stuff, either, though Gaga has expressed a personal affinity for Rilke. She's said that his "philosophy of solitude" resonates with her, and in August 2009, while on tour in Japan, she tattooed a quote from Rilke's *Letters to a Young Poet* on the inside of her upper left arm: "In the deepest hour of the night, confess to yourself that you would die if you were forbidden to write. And look deep into your heart where it spreads its roots, the answer, and ask yourself, must I write?'" She was shot displaying the fresh ink while walking down the street in a long blond wig streaked with purple and pink.

Her aggressive weirdness spawned an amusing post called "Why Do We Find It So Hard to Like Lady Gaga?" on *New York* magazine's website, which elicited hilariously polarized reactions:

"I just keep getting the impression she's a glorified wannabe," wrote one commenter. "A pastiche of every blonde pop singer we've ever known in recent times, not forgetting Donatella Versace. . . . She lacks genuine mystery and should stop calculating her every move. Will wearing Hussein Chalayan, exaggerated shoulder pads and wigs buy her genuine credibilty?"

"I find it hard to like her because I don't think she is a 'bona fide eccentric,'" wrote another. "She's trying too hard to come off that way, she wears stuff that's all been done before

(Christ, even someone as mainstream as Beyoncé wears 'crazy' metallic dresses) and the teacup-carrying bullshit is so self-consciously an attempt to get attention. In her interview with Jonathan Ross last week she actually tried to claim that lighting hairspray on fire as a 'performance artist' was in some way controversial."

A dissenter: "I like Lady Gaga. Her music videos are fun to watch when I'm on the elliptical. And I like her style, regardless of whether it's calculated or coming from a completely organic place. If more pop stars and starlets made an effort to present themselves as unique and eccentric, pop culture would be more interesting."

And someone sure of how it would all end: "She's from Yonkers with a fake Euro accent! She might have talent but she made herself into a gimmick as the girl who wears no pants and makes songs for me to dance to while I'm drunk in the club. The whole façade will die out in a year or two like the rest of them."

In 2008, newly signed to Island Def Jam, Gaga and Fusari took a trip to Miami to meet with Tom Lord-Alge, a Grammy-winning producer and mixer. They wanted him to mix "Beautiful, Dirty, Rich"—Gaga and Fusari both thought it had the potential to be her first single, but not as it was. Starland recalls being dubious, but once Lord-Alge got hold of it, she knew it was a contender. "He created breaks in the song that really made it a lot better than it was," she says. "He did an awesome job." As for Fusari and Gaga's personal relationship, says Starland,

"They were very, very tight at that point. So tight. They were so excited when they came back."

Not long after that, Island Def Jam dropped Gaga. "L.A. Reid heard 'Disco Heaven' and 'Beautiful, Dirty, Rich'—he heard those tracks and made the slit-the-knife-across-the-throat motion and cut her loose," says Brendan Sullivan.

One source remains perplexed, to this day, by the decision to drop her: "When she would come into the office, it would buzz *crazy* for her." Josh Sarubin was her biggest champion, pushing her in meetings. He was, according to Starland, left out of the loop about the decision to drop Gaga. "Josh was in a regular A&R meeting, and they were listing off acts they dropped that week, and they said, '. . . and Lady Gaga,'" says Starland. "He found out, in front of everyone at this meeting, that they had dropped her without L.A. Reid even telling him."

One source thinks that Reid didn't understand who Lady Gaga's audience was: "When you're running a record label, you want to be very familiar with the audience you are selling your music to, and you want to be on the same level as what your artist is trying to convey," says the source. "It would've been a disservice to keep her around and not know how to market her properly. If she had stayed on Island Def Jam with someone that didn't really understand the vision, she might not have done so well."

Sullivan agrees; he says if she'd stayed signed to IDJ, she'd be a niche artist eking out a living. "I love La Roux"—the band led by an androgynous Brit singer whose sound is similar to Gaga's, although her voice is wispier and sparser—"but she would basically have been like La Roux. She'd be playing the third-largest venue in lots of cities—like the Bowery Ballroom in New York. She wouldn't be Lady Gaga, and her songs would have lacked the maturity that [she's] going to get to, that make them so appealing."

Of course, to Gaga, it wasn't easy to be that forward-thinking and philosophical. To her credit, she tried.

Her personal life, too, was a mess.

"Her relationship with Rob became very touch and go," Starland recalls, "and she started to get involved with Lüc. He was very cute, and she used to get very nervous to see him. She'd say, 'Oh my God, Wendy, you don't understand how nervous I am, he's a big deal, he's a bartender down here, he's 'in the scene.'" She chuckles. "This was 'in-the-scene' Lüc."

After the twin disappointments of getting dropped by her label and realizing that Fusari was not an option, Lüc was a good distraction. She'd had a traumatic confrontation with Fusari's fiancée, who had point-blank asked the two if she could trust them to be alone together. They both replied, "No." Jane told Gaga, "You're not a friend." Fusari began sleeping on the couch in his studio, talked about moving in with Stefani in New York. Starland thinks that Fusari's situation suddenly seemed too complicated and heavy for Stefani; Sullivan thinks she really wanted nothing more to do with him. "You see the age difference between her and Fusari," he says. "You can understand what's going on there."

Lüc, by comparison, was hot, popular, and he chose her. It boosted her ego, even if he often didn't treat her so well.

Gaga's friends during this time period say that although Lüc and Gaga were definitely a couple, Lüc wasn't faithful.

He'd also put her down, mocking her taste in music, telling her she was way too driven. His unappealing behavior would inspire some of the most amusing—and biggest—singles on *The Fame*. Most of them didn't get written till after their breakup, and even then Gaga had to be pushed. At first, says Sullivan, she was afraid to: "She said, 'I can't. It'll be like sealing the envelope. Writing about my breakup with Lüc will just make it real.'"

Once she started, she couldn't stop. "Poker Face," says Sullivan, is not, as she has said, about her fantasizing about a woman while having sex with a man. It's far more prosaic: After they broke up, still tormented, Gaga asked Sullivan if he thought she should go down to the bar where Lüc worked and try to talk to him. "I'm telling her she should just be cool, be seen all over town being totally fine without him," he says. "I'm telling her, 'You don't understand how it works with a guy like Lüc. You've got to show him your poker face.' She laughs a little bit. I go, 'What?' She goes, 'Nothing. Nothing.'"

"Summer Boy," says Sullivan, was Gaga ruminating about the chances of a future with Lüc, and realizing: no. He was good for sex and fun and driving around town in his El Camino, but even though she loved him, it was a lost cause. "Boys Boys Boys," says Sullivan, "is about her date with Lüc Carl on March 23, 2007, to go see the Killers at Madison Square Garden."

Lüc had very specific tastes. Some might call them limited. "Lüc didn't like pop music, so Lüc basically didn't respect anything she did," Sullivan says. "He just liked hair metal. It was the only thing he wanted to play. Anyway, this is her first big date with Lüc—they've been dating for about three months at this point, but this is the first time they have a night out together. They get dressed up, they go uptown to see the Killers, Lüc gets these awful seats way up in the bleachers."

Gaga writes about going to see that show—leaving out the part about the surly boyfriend—in "Boys Boys Boys."

"I went in wanting to write the girl version of Mötley Crüe's 'Girls, Girls, Girls,'" she said. "I wanted it to sound like AC/DC's 'T.N.T'"—with its refrain, "Oi! Oi! Oi!"—"but with my pop twist. I wanted to write a pop song that this guy I liked, who was a metalhead, would like."

She also references the after-party that Sullivan DJ'd at the Lower East Side's Motor City Bar, a heavy-metal dive with tires for tables, black paint on the walls, and one of the most expansive selections of cheap beer south of 14th Street. "That was really funny, because this one girl showed up literally with a brick of blow, like it's wrapped in tinfoil," he says. "A friend of mine goes in for it, and it's completely fake, like a brick of baking soda!" He says Gaga went nowhere near it.

"Stef didn't do drugs at that time because Lüc . . . he doesn't do drugs, he doesn't have tattoos, and he told her flat-out when they started dating, 'I'm not going to date you if you're a cokehead.' So she kind of left her Upper West Side NYU dropout friends and completely stopped doing blow. And started dating Lüc Carl. That was her life."

Gaga, way later, would admit that she knew she was in love with someone who wasn't supportive of her career and ambition. She has described "Paparazzi" as about her fear that she could have love or a successful career, but not both. She and Lüc would eventually break up and make up several times, and every time they broke up, Sullivan says, he'd take her to some dive bar on the Lower East Side and get her drunk. "She'd, like, slam her beer down after listing, like, ten things about how he doesn't understand anything," says Sullivan. "Like, 'That fucking guy!'

"The concept she came up with," he continues, "is that she's working hard on her music to impress this guy, but the harder she works on the music, the more it will take her away from this guy. So she wins and loses either way."

FIVE

DITCHED

All those problems with Lüc would transpire over the next few months. In March 2007, Gaga was still grappling with getting dropped from Island Def Jam. "I was one of the first people she spoke to when she got dropped," says another old friend, who is no longer in contact with Gaga but retains great affection for her. "She was really sad. She felt totally defeated. But it was amazing, because at the same time, she was still just about keeping this composure, that this was just a bump in the road. She was really honest about how sad she was—it's a blow to the ego, it makes you feel bad when people don't think you're great."

"She's crying her eyes out, she's more depressed than anything in her life," says Sullivan. "It's the worst thing that had ever happened to her. The second worst thing that ever happened to her."

What was the first?

"Oh, her sister fell out of a tree when they were kids and broke her arm. They're really close. Anyway, she's twenty years old, and she has this deal with her father that if she doesn't have a record deal by the time she's twenty, she'll give up. Now she's twenty, and she doesn't have her deal anymore. She's really, really sad."

"It was the worst day of my life," Gaga has said, adding that she drank and drugged her way through it. According to Sullivan, though, she and her father were all business. "In one of those rare but amazing dad moves, her father came downtown" after hearing how upset she was. "He starts to get very Italian about it, very, like, 'Nobody does this to my daughter.' So he says, 'Let me see what I can do.'"

In the end, Gaga took advantage of a loophole in her contract that required Island Def Jam to pay her if they did not release the record.

"I remember thinking," Sullivan says, "that it was the 'Courtney Love Does the Math' deal."

In May of 2000, Courtney Love gave a speech at the Digital Hollywood online entertainment conference in New York City; it was a sensation and later ran, in its entirety, on Salon .com as an essay entitled "Courtney Love Does the Math." In it, Love not only excoriated the record industry for its fear of the Internet and its refusal to embrace the future; she also called them glorified slave-owners for their financial exploitation of artists. It was the latter point that made headlines: She did the math, explaining how a band made up of four members, working with an advance of $1 million, would most likely, and through no fault of their own, wind up netting $45,000 each over the course of twelve months, while the label proportionally grossed $11 million and netted $6 million.

"The system's set up so almost nobody gets paid," Love said. Lady Gaga, at twenty years old, was well aware.

In the wake of the Island Def Jam fiasco, Fusari called his friend Vincent Herbert, who had his own label, Da Family, under the umbrella of Interscope Records; Herbert had given Fusari his first big break, hiring him to produce Destiny's Child. His track record since had been unassailable.

"Rob made just one call to Vincent," says Starland. "He said, 'I've got this artist; you've got to do this for me,'" she says. "It was like, 'I scratch your back, you scratch mine.' They were like, 'OK.' She got her masters back because of Rob, she got her publishing deal with Rob's company, and she got her second record deal because of Rob."

Producer Martin Kierszenbaum, a then-thirty-five-year-old exec at Interscope who also goes by "Cherry Cherry Boom Boom," auditioned her. He assigned Gaga a track to write to, to come up with lyrics and a hook. "All of a sudden, she's visualizing her stardom like no other," says Starland. "She knows she has to make this the song, because it would be in [Kierszenbaum's] best interests to push it."

Gaga ran versions of the track she was working on for Kierszenbaum—which she knew was not just a test but *the* test—past family and friends, soliciting and incorporating feedback relentlessly. Starland was surprised when Gaga played the finished track for her. "The lyrics say, 'Family, doing it for the family,'" she says. "And I go, 'Isn't that the name of your record label?'"

The record label ended up with a new name: Streamline. The song Gaga worked on became "The Fame." (Eventually, Gaga would be signed to three labels under the Interscope umbrella: Streamline, Cherrytree, and Kon Live, with the head of each label getting a piece of her profits.)

DITCHED

It was apparent to Interscope execs that Gaga was special: She could sing, play, write. But her presentation was still a problem. Unless and until that was resolved, she was best kept in the background as a songwriter.

"Interscope is a long, long road which actually involves a lot of people thinking she's great to have around, but not pretty enough to be a pop star," says Sullivan.

"I can speak to this, having sat through many marketing meetings where this project was discussed," says an industry source who wishes to remain unnamed. He was familiar with what he calls "her coffeehouse schtick," via the YouTube clips of her early performances at the Bitter End and her NYU talent competition.

She was conscripted to write songs for other artists, most especially the Pussycat Dolls, for whom she also had to provide reference vocals—basically, she'd have to sing the song so they'd know how to do it themselves. "Gaga doesn't take the Pussycat Dolls very seriously," says her friend Sullivan.

She was cranky. She got into a fight with Lüc, who was angry that this new assignment was cutting into their vacation time. According to Sullivan, Lüc had saved up money to take her on this romantic trip she'd wanted, and now she was, he thought, capriciously cutting it short because her label called with an assignment, and when they called, she went running. Lüc thought she was a spoiled rich girl with no respect for how hard he had to work, and she thought he was an underachiever who didn't understand her drive and didn't support her ambition. This is when she famously told him, "Someday, when we're not together, you won't be able to order a cup of coffee at the fucking deli without hearing or seeing me."

At this point, says the exec, her look was still a detriment. "She had the bikini or the G-string," he says. He's convinced that having been signed by Vincent Herbert was a key factor in the label's decision to start throwing money and muscle behind her.

"Not only does Vincent have a real good ear," he says, "but he has a sense of creating a lane for her—not being excessive in terms of spending millions and millions of dollars on videos, just making sure that she has the [resources] to be what she wants to be."

Note that he says "what" and not "who." It's always been about *what* Gaga wanted to be: the biggest star in the world. Who she would become—this avant-garde freak show who would work for days on end crafting the perfect dance song despite wanting to be taken seriously as a singer-songwriter—was, she saw, merely a vessel to get her to the what.

She used her fight with Lüc over the aborted vacation as material for her Pussycat Dolls assignment. She wound up writing "Money Honey," in which she's telling her boyfriend that the only currency that matters to her is love. Sullivan remembers the first time she played it for him. "I said, 'That's [the name of] an Elvis song.'" She didn't seem to know what he was talking about: "She said, 'Whatever.'"

Then, Sullivan says, Akon—one of Interscope's best-selling artists with his own imprint, a Senegalese singer-songwriter-producer who broke through in 2004 with his debut single "Locked Up"—heard "Money Honey."

"And he realizes," says Sullivan, "there's no reason to buy this song and have the Pussycat Dolls sing it when it's definitely her song and she'd be fantastic at it. That's when he starts pushing her forward as an artist."

At Interscope, her manager Besencon got Gaga a slot at 2007's Lollapalooza. It was at this point, according to Fusari's lawsuit, that he began to get frozen out by Besencon and Gaga. "This is such a music industry thing," says Josh Grier, an entertainment lawyer who represents Wilco and Ryan Adams. "The part that rings really true" about Fusari's lawsuit, Grier says, is the allegation that "Fusari's manager [Besencon] sees where the real talent is, so he goes and fucks his own artist. He gets in bed with her figuratively and makes a separate deal with her and throws Fusari under the bus. That's the part I believe completely."

The Lollapooza booking did not rattle Gaga; if anything, she thought she'd emerge as one of the most buzzed-about new acts on the bill. Once the biggest, most influential rock festival in the country—if not the Western world—Lollapalooza was a nationwide tour founded by Jane's Addiction frontman Perry Farrell in 1991, as alternative music was cresting and taking over the mainstream. The idea was to mash up genres—hip-hop, electronica, industrial, and post-punk acts were all on the bill—and offer downtime activities, like tattooing and body-piercing, on the grounds. But by 1997, Lollapalooza had lost all relevance; Kurt Cobain was long-dead; alternative culture had become so mainstream as to be nullified; and the charts were dominated by boy-bands ('N Sync, Backstreet Boys) and tween-age Disney-bred acts (Christina Aguilera, Britney Spears, Mandy Moore).

It fell apart in 1998, when organizers couldn't book a headliner, and has since been supplanted, in revenue and relevance, by the annual three-day Coachella music festival in California, which was founded in 1999 and took a more holistic approach to booking acts. Coachella did and does still feel alternative, but the roster of acts in any given year has a sense of the music obsessive's abandon: The 2010 line-up included Jay-Z, Radiohead's Thom Yorke, MGMT, Sly and the Family Stone, LCD Soundsystem, Brit ska-punk legends the Specials, and nineties alternative heroes Pavement.

By 2003, Farrell, partnering with Capital Sports & Entertainment, now C3 Presents, was able to revive Lollapalooza by following the Coachella model—a one-off multiday music festival in a fixed location: Chicago. So Gaga's booking, in summer 2007, was, contextually, a low-profile gig—she wasn't even second stage, which is the smaller alternative to whatever's happening on the big stage. She was booked on one of the *smaller* smaller stages—the apportionment of acts at a music festival can resemble nothing so much as the sonic equivalent of a nesting doll—called the BMI stage for its sponsor, Broadcast Music, Inc.

"Basically, we look for people who are just getting started who we think are interesting," says Huston Powell, the promoter at C3 Productions who signed Gaga to Lollapalooza. "It's not too much rocket science."

The headliners on that year's bill were Pearl Jam, Daft Punk, and Muse. Even though this was the biggest booking she'd had to date, Gaga took a very small coterie along: Fusari, a high school pal who was dying to go, and Lady Starlight, who was going to DJ.

Gaga's slot was scheduled for day two, August 4, 2007. The sun was still out when she took the stage. As far as she was concerned, it did not go well. She was repeatedly mistaken for Amy Winehouse, which had one benefit: She got a lot of attention from the paparazzi. Starland maintains there was nothing calculated about Gaga's resemblance to Winehouse, who'd become one of the biggest stars of the year with *Back to Black,* a broken-soul break-up record shot through with narcotized grief. Like Gaga's debut, it smashed all demographics.

"Tons of reporters were charging after her, going, 'Amy Winehouse, Amy Winehouse, we want your comment on this,'" Starland recalls. "And she was like, 'Oh my God, this is awful.' She did not want that at all." That's not to say she wasn't highly aware of what her more successful peers were doing: Lily Allen, like Winehouse, was another distinctive-looking brunette, a foul-mouthed, hard-drinking Brit who'd had massive crossover success with her dub-tinged single "Smile." "When Lily was big," says Starland, "she'd say, 'I need to keep my eye on her; there's only room for one.'"

At sound check, the DJ stand was wobbly, so Gaga asked Besencon to find a replacement that was sturdy. Instead, he improvised a solution, jury-rigging the too-short leg. During the performance, Starlight's record kept skipping, and the folding stage kept bouncing every time she'd jump. "She and Starlight just kind of showed up and were like, 'We're going to show these people what New York City's about,'" Sullivan says. "And that's not what you do at an outdoor show."

Gaga plowed through anyway, this goth-looking chick singing dance music in a black bikini top and working her stripper
moves in the sunlight, turning her back to the audience and
bending over in her thong. It was confusing.

"She seemed to go for it from the get-go," says C3's Powell
of her set. "Sometimes those are difficult slots, but she seemed
to be very sure of herself. She had a lot of people watching her;
they were pretty intrigued by it." He estimates that there were
75,000 people on the ground total; a fraction of that—which
turned out to be about 200—was still the biggest crowd for
which she'd ever performed.

"She was on the smallest stage outside the kiddie area," says
Quinn Donahue, talent buyer at C3 Presents. Donahue helped
Gaga set up and was surprised that she only had her manager
and her DJ in tow. "I remember them cutting it kinda close" to
set time, he says. He helped with the turntables and mixers,
calling the minimal prep time "throw-and-go."

Like Powell, Donahue was familiar with Gaga only through
MySpace; he says he had no idea what to expect. There was
nothing about her sound that really fit the Lollapalooza brand—
it was "more pop"—but her stage presence was undeniable.
"She had the charisma," says Donahue, who watched her forty-
five-minute set. "Once the crowd warmed up to her, they were
all about it. She just kind of stole [the show]."

Sullivan says Gaga did not have the same experience. "They
go onstage and have every technical problem imaginable," he
says. "She almost didn't want to talk about it when she got back."
But apparently, she did: "First of all," says Sullivan, "there's the
music, which was not where it is today. She's got Rob Fusari's

beats. Second problem: She could not get past how out-of-place she seemed. "She's in a bikini but she's behind a synthesizer, which isn't exactly sexy."

All Gaga could really think about, however, was the shaky table and the record that kept skipping because of it. "She spoke to the direct head of her label, Vincent Herbert," says Starland. "And Vincent said to her, 'You know what you've got to do.' And Laurent was gone the next day."

So was Starlight, axed as DJ, though her firing was much gentler: Gaga framed it as a lateral move, to stylist. And that, says Sullivan, "was the beginning of her and me working together more. I knew automatically. I love Starlight to death, but as a DJ—I would never let a record skip. I was like, I would've seen that coming."

One of the headliners at Lollapalooza 2010: Lady Gaga. Actually, with the announcement that her stage set was going to cost $150,000, she declared herself *the* headliner.

After Lollapalooza, it was back to writing, recording, and attempting to streamline the Gaga image. She was still unable to divine a clear aesthetic, still working her heavy-metal-stripper look for lack of another idea. Gaga knew that she needed to look extreme, but right now she still looked like something out of *Vice* magazine's "Don't" pages—vicious street fashion commentary by New York City's most acidic hipsters.

Her first priority, though, was getting herself on Jimmy Iovine's radar. The fifty-seven-year-old Iovine is the head of Interscope, which he cofounded in 1990. He'd produced records for U2, Patti Smith, Tom Petty & the Heartbreakers; he also coproduced *8 Mile,* the critically acclaimed hip-hopera starring Eminem and based on the rapper's life.

"In his area—the creation of pop/hip-hop/R&B—he's considered an expert," says a veteran of the industry. "The conflict with Jimmy becomes—the guy who [worked with] John Lennon, Tom Petty, Stevie Nicks—there's this expectation that he'd be an 'artist guy'"—the kind of exec that cultivates talent over the long term, who can help develop and sustain a body of work.

"But he's not," continues the source. "You'd think with that reputation that this is a guy who'd understand everything from Grizzly Bear to Beck, but in truth, this is a guy who's all about the hit single." When approached by Iovine about working with Akon, this source says he was reluctant to recommend the idea to his artist. But he did, and the project was successful. "I have no problem telling Jimmy, 'That was all you,'" says the source. "We didn't see it. But hey man, that was [Akon] completely, that launched our single and our tour. One hundred percent him. We didn't see the depth in him as an artist, but Jimmy did."

"Jimmy is the wizard behind the curtain for any act on Universal [Interscope's parent company]," says Wendy Starland. "Every artist goes into a deal thinking they're going to get the push, but the label really only has enough money to push a couple of artists [a year]."

One version of events has Iovine in his office on a Sunday afternoon, spinning stuff for Akon, soliciting his feedback. Iovine pops in "Boys, Boys, Boys" by Gaga, and Akon tells Iovine that he likes it. A lot. "So Jimmy Iovine calls her on a Sunday

afternoon," says a source, "and goes, 'Stefani, Gaga, whatever—
I just want you to know that we really like this song of yours,
and we're going to be behind you.' And that was the moment
they decided that all the money and all the resources would go
towards pushing Lady Gaga. All because Akon"—who'd long
believed in her potential—"said he liked it."

Akon has called Lady Gaga his "franchise player." He's
said that she's making it possible for him to consider retiring
early, and upon hearing Gaga for the first time, he told Iovine,
"Yo, I want to sign that right there. She needs to be under my
umbrella"—Kon Live, the label he ran under Interscope. Iovine's
response, Akon has said, was "Yeah, whatever you want. Take
her. Let's get it done."

In Gaga, they had an artist who, thanks to her ill-fated deal
with Island Def Jam, had a good chunk of album-ready material in mastered form. But she still needed to write half a record, and the stuff that wasn't working for her, or for Iovine
and Akon, would go to other artists: the Pussycat Dolls, New
Kids on the Block, and her teenage heroine Britney Spears, who
recorded a track Gaga cowrote called "Quicksand."

"They'd rejected so many songs and so many styles at that
point—so much," says Brendan Sullivan. "And she was writing
for the Pussycat Dolls before that, but even then, they were
disappointed in her and had rejected songs."

It was, Gaga knew, another pivotal moment, akin to the
pressure she felt when writing "The Fame" for Vincent Herbert.
Her version of writing "Just Dance" is glamorous in its rock 'n'

roll decadence. She gets off a flight from New York to L.A., hungover from her going-away party on the Lower East Side the night before (she's relocated to L.A. indefinitely) and heads straight to the recording studio where, minutes later, out pours the song, an ode to drinking and dancing, nothing more.

But Sullivan—who, like many friends, recalls a girl so driven she rarely indulged in alcohol, let alone drugs—suspects she applied herself with the same rigor and discipline when it came to penning a surefire hit, a song that would make Interscope move fast to make her a star.

Starland, meanwhile, was still hoping that Gaga would, as she saw it, do right by her. She'd spent Christmas 2007 with Gaga's family on the Upper West Side; she says Gaga was upset that Rob Fusari, who'd promised to come, never showed up. Starland says Gaga told her she had a special gift for her, and presented her with a Chanel 2.55 bag worth several thousand dollars. It was understood, Starland says, that this also doubled as payment for Starland's role in her career, for discovering her and introducing her to Fusari. Starland says she eventually worked up the nerve to confront Gaga over dinner one night at Tao, an expensive Asian fusion restaurant in midtown Manhattan. Gaga paid.

"I said, 'Stefani, you only know how valuable a relationship or a contact is in someone's life when it's taken away.' And she's like, 'Since I don't have a lot of money right now, next time I won't give you a bag, I'll give you a vacation.' And I just said to her, 'Honestly, are you planning on screwing me over? Where would you be without all of this effort and development and connections?' And she was like, 'Wendy, our relationship is such that I would give you a vacation or whatever, but if you want to put this down with our lawyers, we will never talk again. Our friendship will be over.'" Starland opted not to sue—it's not her style, she says—but the friendship remained distant and strained.

Not long after her dinner with Starland, on the Friday before Valentine's Day, 2008, Gaga presented "Just Dance" to Interscope. "Jimmy Iovine is known for having these meetings—he's like Steve Jobs—where he makes everyone sit and wait until he's ready," says Sullivan. "And it's either because 'None of you are doing your jobs, and I don't know why I hired any of you people, and you people don't even like music in the first place,' blah blah blah, or he's making them wait because he's heard something and he wants them to get on it right away."

On this day, according to Sullivan, it was the latter. "He heard 'Just Dance,' and he was like, 'This is a hit record, and this is the one we've been waiting for since we signed her.'" Iovine brought Gaga into the office, into that meeting. "He said, 'You did it, you did everything we asked you to do. We believed in you and we didn't know why, and now we know why.' And he played the song for the whole office, and she danced on the table. On the boardroom table." Not long after, Iovine had her relocate to L.A. to finish the album.

As Sullivan later wrote in an essay for *Esquire* magazine's May 2010 "Women" issue, Gaga had returned to New York for a visit and she and Sullivan were eating lunch in a Midtown deli when she got a call from Bert Padell, Madonna's former business manager. He told her he wanted to step in and take over;

she couldn't believe it. He was one of the many high-level people she'd auditioned for as a teenager.

"Her dad's a very savvy businessman," says Sullivan. "He can basically get a meeting with anyone." Her mother's savvy as well; before the Padell audition she'd done her homework and learned that he wrote poetry, and at the audition she asked him about it. He gave her a copy of his book of poems. After Stefani performed, Padell said to her, 'Well, you know, good luck with everything. We'll call you.'" And he'd finally called. Stefani, now Gaga, said to him, "Actually, we have met. My mother still has your book of poetry." She told Sullivan that it was "the best phone call of my entire life."

Her boyfriend Lüc, however, was ever more unhappy. "Lüc never gave up on his rock 'n' roll fantasy world, even though he'd never made it as a drummer," says Sullivan. "He thought having a girlfriend with a record deal would be VIP shows and instant status. He didn't know that music was an actual profession and that he would have a busy girl who was always out of town or on her BlackBerry."

By that December, she'd had enough. After getting into a fight with Lüc one night over her needing to work and him complaining that she was neglecting him for the sake of her career, she told him: "I want you to get my self-tanner, my lipstick, and my disco ball, because you and I are through."

SIX

ONE SEQUIN AT A TIME

aga had been building a solid, substantial fan base online, which sounds far easier than it actually is; if anything, the Internet fractures attention spans and creates split-second, evanescent phenomena. Far more rare is the artist or clip that originates on the Web and becomes massively impactful, that moves into the more traditional mediums of TV, magazines, newspapers, that becomes known even to those people who don't have a computer.

Susan Boyle, who became a global phenomenon months before Gaga herself did, is that similar, rare example: Her performance on Simon Cowell's UK show, *Britain's Got Talent*, shot around the Web at warp speed, and a confluence of factors—Boyle's personal story, the production values of the clip, the meta-narrative of a homely spinster singing a song about daring to dream, charming a skeptical audience and the famously cruel Cowell—has turned her, eighteen months later, into a multimillionaire.

Gaga had none of these known quantities: She wasn't framed by an existing structure, such as *American Idol*. Her presentation was deliberately confusing and a bit menacing; Boyle was a middle-aged woman who lived alone with her cat and said she'd never been in love. Gaga, unlike Boyle, had no machine behind her, no context. Though Boyle seemed, too, to be an overnight sensation, the clip from *Britain's Got Talent* that made her a superstar played like a mini-movie, the quintessential underdog story told in about seven minutes. Gaga was selling a first single that, without visuals, was utterly indistinguishable from the bulk of preexisting, slickly produced, Auto-Tuned pop; she was trying to carve an identity for herself in a super-cluttered landscape. (Fittingly, Boyle and Gaga have expressed an interest in collaborating.)

And yet, this is Gaga's genius: "She's struck this difficult balance; she's both intimate and enigmatic with her fan base," says Eric Garland, CEO of BigChampagne.com. "Technologies like Twitter and Facebook and MySpace have created these platforms for 'mass intimacy,' but mostly it doesn't work very well, mostly because you know that I'm not talking to *you*—if I wanted to talk to you, I'd call or e-mail. When you're speaking to ten million 'friends,' you don't have that intimacy. But some artists can make that happen—like in live performances, where people in the cheap seats feel like they're having a command performance. An artist like Lady Gaga feels like she's doing that, on the Internet, in real time. That's very difficult."

In May 2010, a YouTube clip of a twelve-year-old boy performing an astonishing cover of Gaga's "Paparazzi" became a viral phenomenon, generating more than eighteen million views. Within days, sixth-grader Grayson Chance was on *The Ellen DeGeneres Show*, where he took a call from Lady Gaga herself, who gushed over his abilities and then helped him secure a record deal. Full circle.

Like every other arm of old media—network television,

radio, publishing—the record industry has been grappling with maintaining both pop-cultural relevance and profit margins in the Internet age, and though a company like Interscope has the infrastructure to create a Lady Gaga, that alone is no longer enough.

"The process of breaking a star has become very difficult," says an unnamed source familiar with Interscope's Gaga strategy. "We used to have a very push-through relationship with the music consumer, where you got it on the radio and the radio pounded it one hundred times a day, and the kids said, 'It must be a hit,' and went out and bought it. The consumer now, kids thirteen to twenty-two years old, they're much more savvy. They have many more sources of information. They don't just listen to the radio and say, 'If Ryan Seacrest says it's a hit, it's got to be a hit.' They're forming their own judgments. To break an artist today, there's got to be some grist for the presentation. Enter Lady Gaga."

"Lady Gaga is probably the greatest artist development story we've seen in memorable history," says James Diener, CEO and president of A&M/Octone records. It wasn't all her—she could not have broken through without the investment and support of a major label—but she worked harder than most.

The industry, Garland says, "should give her a big hug and tens of millions of dollars. You couldn't ask for a better partner at this moment in the business."

The next part of the prerelease strategy was establishing Gaga not only in the gay community but as *of* it—if she did break out, she would not only have a committed core of consumers with highly disposable income, but she'd have cred as an outsider artist, despite her highly commercial sound. Interscope hired FlyLife, a NYC-based public relations company specializing in the gay marketplace, to book Gaga into the right nightclubs, get DJs to spin her record, hook her up with the right people. "They were definitely, really specifically trying to push her toward a gay audience," says the rapper Cazwell, who was outsourced by FlyLife to perform with her.

Iovine had also decided he was going to book Gaga at Miami's dance-centric Winter Music Conference, March 25–29, 2008, and that she'd perform whether or not he could secure the proper permits from the city. Sullivan recalls the exact circumstances; he consults his electronic diary for the date and time.

"On March 1, yeah on March 1 at 2:43 P.M., I text her, saying, 'Are you going to be home for your birthday?'" he recalls. "And she calls me back right away and goes, 'No, I don't think we're going to be home for my birthday. Jimmy wants to push us forward so we can go to the Winter Music Conference and meet all the DJs and industry people and have them hear our new record, and if that goes well we're going to go directly to Los Angeles and film the video for 'Just Dance.'"

Gaga was calm; this was what she had been working for, toward, what she expected. Sullivan was shocked. "I was like, 'Holy shit, OK!' We'd just gone from nobody coming to our shows unless we texted them to getting flown to Miami."

It was a microcosmic version of Gaga's ultimate trajectory: seemingly going nowhere one minute, suddenly everywhere.

◆ ◆ ◆

Despite playing to such a tech-savvy crowd, there's not much of Gaga's WMC performance online, just a quick, grainy clip with low sound quality, and a ten-minute interview that looks like it was done for cable access. She is wearing what she calls "disco panties"—they look as if they were constructed from the mirrored tiles of a disco ball—a billowing white pirate top, and sunglasses. Her newly blond hair is frizzy and flyaway; she struggles constantly to keep her bangs matted to her forehead. Gaga is telling the interviewer about her label head Jimmy Iovine's love for her.

"I'm the kind of girl he takes to the prom," she says. "I'm quirky, I'm from Brooklyn"—that's a lie—"I'm Italian." She is also charming, explaining her raison d'être: "Changing the world, one sequin at a time." She is compact, throaty, and with her New York dialect—soft Ts and slightly drawn-out vowels— she very much looks and sounds, incredibly, like the relentlessly chipper TV chef Rachael Ray.

The first show Gaga played at WMC was during the day, on the roof of the Raleigh Hotel, a swank four-star owned by the hotelier Andre Balazs, himself a huge nightlife fixture and gossip-column staple in New York (best known, perhaps, for his one-time engagement to Uma Thurman). It was a bit thrown together. "We didn't have money for costumes," says Sullivan. "The backup dancers each got about one hundred bucks per show. None of us made any money." Still, they did what they could: They had smoke machines, lights, and disco balls. "We lit hairspray on fire," he recalls. "We had fun."

ONE SEQUIN AT A TIME

Interscope had hired Coalition Media Group to promote Gaga; Coalition had also helped break the Scissor Sisters, booking them into gay parties and clubs. "They booked us into a gay club called Score in the middle of Miami, and the gay dudes just loved us," Sullivan says. "We'd done the hipster shoe-gaze, eye-roll downtown scene, and we didn't want to do that. We wanted to play in the gay market, the kind of big, crazy clubs where they would accept us. And that was pretty much our biggest show; we just nailed it that night. And then we went back to our hotel, showered, and flew to L.A. to film the video for 'Just Dance.'"

This, too, was ultra-low-budget. "We had to park at Martin Luther King and Crenshaw Boulevard, which sounds like a Chris Rock joke," says Sullivan. "We rented this guy's terribly tacky house for the video. It looks like somebody's 'my-parents-are-out-of-town' party in Jersey or something." Sullivan recalls the shoot as chaotic and thoroughly unglamorous. "We're, like, throwing champagne on the shag carpet, jumping on the furniture, and walking on the coffee table," he says. "And then they'd be like, 'CUT!' and we'd sit down and breathe for a second, and this weird guy would come from around the corner and be like, 'Don't sit on the arm of the sofa; it's not good for it.' Ha ha."

In her retelling, Gaga was characteristically hyperbolic, comparing it, in one interview, to "being on a Martin Scorsese set." But she did have a manicure that gave her nails the appearance of being sheathed in fishnet, which was a stroke of genius.

She was now living full-time in L.A., trying to finish the album, but it was around the time of the "Just Dance" video shoot that she met a New York–based photographer named Warwick Saint, who shot her for potential album artwork. He was brought in by Gaga's new manager, Troy Carter, whom she hired when she signed to Interscope. An African-American powerhouse, Carter is actually quite tiny, maybe a little over five feet. He kept a low public profile; his other clients included Freeway and Eve.

Gaga and Saint had their first meeting over a beer one night at the House of Blues. "She was quite sexy," he says. "But it wasn't out-there in terms of clothes." Gaga was, he says, wearing jeans, a loose T-shirt, and reading glasses. He found her highly mature for her age: "Super-smart, super-bright, super-creative," he says. "She often spoke about her family and her dad." She seemed, he says, "to have a good relationship with her father."

The label had set up a shoot at a downtown L.A. spot called the Bordello bar; it was to go from six in the morning till four in the afternoon. He recalls being underwhelmed by her stylist, whose work for Gaga he found "costume-y," and he recommended a friend named Martina Nilsson to Carter and Gaga; Nilsson soon took over. "After the meeting," he says, "Gaga was like, 'Of course. She just, like, totally gets me.' And Martina was on the job straightaway."

From the moment the shoot began (with her own music on the sound system), Gaga was in complete command, which Saint says is unusual. "Some artists you put in front of the camera— it's like trying to suck blood from a stone," he says. "Lady Gaga was a performer from the get-go, which, for a photographer, is a dream. She would, like, flip upside down and do these cool body positions. She loved being in front of the camera. She loved being the center of attention."

After the shoot, Saint invited Gaga to come look at the images: "I was like, 'It's a good idea for you to see what you're like in front of the camera.'" For all her bravado on the set, he says "she had a bit of a complex about her nose. She was considering having it done, but I told her not to."

Aliya Naumoff, who was hired to shoot the first performance Lady Gaga did for Interscope execs (it's known as a showcase, and in this instance it was so that others in corporate would know what they were selling), recalls seeing no outward signs of insecurity on Gaga's part, and thinking how unusual that was. The show was on a rooftop in midtown Manhattan; Gaga had two backup dancers and didn't seem too familiar with them, but "she was full of confidence; I was kind of blown away," Naumoff says. "I was like, 'That one is gonna be the next combination of Madonna and Britney.'"

A few nights later, Naumoff went to see Gaga perform at the downtown club Mansion, a low-ceilinged space that's divided into two small rooms. "The club was maybe one-tenth full," Naumoff says. During her set, "everyone was like, 'What is that?' No one was really paying attention." After the performance, Naumoff, who'd had a pleasant working experience with Gaga at that Interscope showcase, went up to Gaga to say hi and congratulations.

"She blew me off; she didn't care," Naumoff says, laughing. "She just didn't give a fuck. I wasn't insulted. I was like, 'She's in it to win it. She's unstoppable.'"

"Just Dance" was released, to little reaction, on April 8. It finally reached the top of the Billboard Hot 100 chart in January 2009. As for Saint, he stayed in sporadic contact with Gaga via text messages: "I'd say, 'Cheers Gaga, I just saw you on . . .' And she'd be like, 'Hey, I got played on the radio in Canada!'" As with her other friends and acquaintances, most exchanges were all about her. "And as she was getting more and more famous, her responses would become less and less frequent," he says.

In April, Wendy Starland—herself newly relocated to L.A.—got a surprise phone call from Gaga. "She said, 'All I want to do is hang out with you. I'm dating this guy, he's my stylist. . . .'" This was Matt Williams, who was Gaga's age and who had recently relocated from New York City. "She's like, 'He's an entrepreneur, too, and people are jealous of him, too, because he's so successful, just like me. I thought I'd give him a shot to do all my styling.'" Gaga told Starland she'd just done an interview with *Rolling Stone* and had given Starland credit for her discovery, and then the topic turned to whether Starland deserved further remuneration for connecting Gaga and Fusari.

According to Starland, Gaga said that the idea of getting paid for introducing one artist to another was a bit much. "She said, 'Someone must have introduced you to Moby'"—whom Starland had worked with on his 2008 album *Last Night,* singing the lead vocal on his single "I'm in Love." Starland countered that, in fact, Moby had found her on MySpace, and that without her help, Gaga might never have made it. The girls never spoke again.

Though she has no problem exerting control, the confrontation with Starland is uncharacteristic; Gaga does not like to cut people out of her life or fire them. In the case of the former, she'll do the slow fade, leaving it to the left-behind party to figure out what's up. In the case of the latter, she'll leave it to someone else to do the firing, or claim no knowledge of what's going on. David Ciemny, who worked as her tour manager for about a year and a half beginning in spring 2008, and took a leave of absence in the fall of '09, says he was confused by her response when he broached the idea of going back out on the road.

"I said, 'I'm ready to go,' but she told me, 'You look different. You're not ready to go back out.' And I'd go, 'Yeah, yeah, I am.' And she'd say, 'I don't think you're ready.' Maybe she'd made up in her mind that she was progressing to a new level. . . ."

After a few months passed, he eventually sent her an e-mail: "I was like, 'You know, Gaga, I don't know if it's you or your manager, but I don't have a job anymore, and my paycheck stopped.'" (She'd kept him on the payroll for three months after he left the tour.) He asked her if he'd been fired, if there was a chance he was going out on her tour in two weeks, where he stood.

She replied quickly, via e-mail. "She said, 'You always have a job with me. I didn't know about this. Let me get on this. Hugs and kisses, Gagaloo.' But that was where it kind of ended. I didn't hear back from her."

Starland wasn't the only problematic person from Gaga's past. After nearly eighteen months of silent estrangement, Rob Fusari filed a $30.5 million lawsuit against Gaga on March 17,

2010. It was a scathing and highly emotional document that revealed the extent of the romantic relationship between the two.

The first page of the suit has a highly unusual "Introduction," marked as such. It opens with a footnoted passage from William Congreve's poem "The Mourning Bride":

> Heaven has no rage like love to hatred turned,
> Nor hell a fury like a woman scorned.

Fusari follows that up with an explanatory note: "All business is personal," he writes. "When these personal relationships evolve into romantic entanglements, any corresponding business relationship usually follows the same trajectory so that when one crashes they all burn. That is what happened here." He went on to allege that he'd only received two royalty checks from Lady Gaga, one for $203,000 and one for $394,965. On the latter, he said, was a note on the back that read, "endorsed in accord and satisfaction of all sums due to undersigned"—meaning that had he signed the check, he would have been signing away all rights to future monies.

On March 19, Gaga filed a countersuit. Meanwhile, Fusari's original lawyer, Robert Meloni, wound up bowing out of the case, subbing in another lawyer from his firm. Gaga's contention was that Fusari was acting as both her agent and manager, which, says a high-profile entertainment lawyer who's gone up against Meloni, violates employment statutes. But what this attorney, who asked to remain unnamed, finds most interesting is that Fusari, the industry veteran, is essentially claiming that this very young girl exploited him.

"Typically, the artist says, 'This guy took advantage of me and shoved this agreement down my throat,'" the attorney says. "It's a little different twist here, where he's saying, 'I would have done this typical deal, [but she and her father] took me down this path and now they're saying, 'Screw you.'"

The overall intent on both sides, she says, was to attract as much media attention as possible—Fusari with the maudlin opening to his complaint, exposing their romantic relationship, and Gaga with her high-profile, immediate countersuit.

Veteran entertainment lawyer Josh Grier believes that, no matter the merits of Fusari's complaint—and he thinks it's reasonable—Gaga will outlast him by sheer dint of her financial resources, even though he thinks her counterclaim is exceptionally weak: "Just denying everything is not enough," he says. That said, she can keep him in litigation longer, cost him more money than he can afford to spend, force him to back down.

"It looks like gamesmanship to me," Grier says. "The game of litigation in the music business—nobody ever goes to trial." He estimates that Fusari spent $25,000 just to file the complaint. "Does he really have the money to [pursue] it?" asks the lawyer. "These litigators are real mercenaries. I expect at some point it'll be settled and you'll go, 'What's the settlement?' and they'll go, 'Sorry, it's confidential.' It's like reading a book, and somebody's torn out the last chapter."

Rob Fusari, at the time of this writing, was still with his fiancée.

SEVEN

"I AM LIVING FOR YOU RIGHT NOW"

*G*aga spent May 2009 playing small gigs in gay clubs, blogging, giving interviews to anyone who asked or answered. She told *HX* magazine that "When I play at gay clubs, it's like playing for my friends; they get it and understand what I'm trying to say." She would later say that she was bisexual and had had relationships with women, but had only ever been in love with men.

"I had a lot of gay friends growing up," she told MTV. "I went to a lot of gay clubs."

That's not true, according to the account she gave in an unpublished interview. She was going to school, to voice lessons, to auditions, and to *TRL* to see Britney.

"I think her whole image as a sort of gay ambassador and gay icon . . . I think she always wants to leave that kind of open," says David Ciemny, her former tour manager. "You know, we all know that she's a girl, she likes guys, that's about all there is to it. Her close girlfriends from high school, they're not lesbians. But, you know, artists who are more mysterious are more appealing anyway."

Later, as she was breaking in the States and drawing comparisons to pop star Katy Perry, who'd just scored a hit with "I Kissed a Girl," Gaga deftly depicted herself as the real thing and Perry as a poseur. "I'm not trying to use my gay fans to get a fan base. I really, genuinely love them. . . . I do not want to make anyone feel used."

One of the first performers Gaga hired, via FlyLife, was the rapper-songwriter–nightlife presence Cazwell, whose outsized sensibility was ideal: He was known, in his scene, for hilariously titled singles such as "All Over Your Face" and "I Seen Beyoncé at Burger King." (His current press photo is Gaga-esque, with blood coming from his nose, smeared all over his chin.)

Cazwell often performed with Amanda Lepore, the subculture's superstar—still, he'd been warned by a FlyLife staffer not to mess up. "They said, 'Lady Gaga, just so you know, she's extremely professional, so be there on time.'" He was hired to rap on a remix of "Just Dance" and to perform with Gaga at a couple of local gigs—one at a now-defunct club on Avenue C and another at a club called Boysroom.

"There were stickers all over [the club] that said, 'Lady Gaga, taking over the world, one sequin at a time,'" says Cazwell. He remembers a nice, polite girl who was nonetheless deadly serious. "We were performing on a stage the size of a door," he says, "but she still had sound check, and she was really specific about the opening and the choreography. She's like, 'At the end of your rap, I want to push you down on your knees and then I'm going to get on top of you,' and she's like, riding me, you know?" He was impressed by her professionalism and decisiveness.

The crowd, Cazwell says, was a combination of "Brooklyn hipsters and downtown gays," and they were not as impressed.

"They were like, 'Oh, that's interesting.' Everyone was just watching with arms crossed. No one bum-rushed her, no one said anything."

Gaga was stalling out a bit: She wasn't getting all that much traction even on the fringes of the mainstream. Alternative publications that would've been natural fits, such as *Nylon, Paper,* and *V* magazine, weren't interested. MTV only played a few hours of music videos a day, in the morning. Interscope was thinking of booking her as an opening act for New Kids on the Block, and whereas another artist who was cultivating an outré persona might have scoffed, she was smart enough to take every opportunity.

She was a genius when it came to the Web and knew she could control her message there. She was tweeting constantly. She solicited the friendship of controversial and snarky gossip blogger Perez Hilton, who has become a celebrity himself and who relentlessly promotes the people he likes. He can be equally tenacious when it comes to denigrating those he does not. Gaga quickly became not only a recurring character but a heroine, and he began calling her his "wife."

"She saw him not only as a spokesman for the gay community, but as an ally to really help launch her career," says David Ciemny. "So this was a calculated friendship and decision from Day One." She invited him to dinner, talked to him on the phone; as her fame grew, she'd invite him to visit her on tour and take him out for mani-pedi dates, which he'd shoot and post to his site. For Halloween last year, he dressed up as Lady Gaga.

"She would send him videos and songs right after she finished them; she'd say, 'This is going to Perez; I don't want anyone else to have it,'" Ciemny says. "And he would give her good reviews; he would never bash Gaga." His access, though, became exponentially less direct. "He would call me," says Ciemny, "because he couldn't get ahold of her."

Hilton's first Gaga post went up June 8, 2008; it was a link to her video for "Just Dance." "Finally, a new artist that explodes onto the scene in America and embraces pop music, like old school Madonna!" he wrote. "'Just Dance' is the lead single off her new album and this shit be our summer anthem!!! You must CLICK HERE to check out the super stylin' and ferosh video. It's like LastNightsParty and The Cobrasnake come to life. The song is sooo damn catchy!"

"She had a very strong sense of how to use the Internet to market her record [before it] was on radio and video play and in public awareness," says James Diener, CEO and president of A&M/Octone. "In 2008, she's very mysterious. You're not quite sure exactly what she looks like, where she is, what this is all about. What you have for her is at least a year of her starting to develop serious traction amongst a grassroots community via the Internet, clubs, DJs, various markets around the world before the United States. There's very, very strong word-of-mouth buzzing about her in the blogosphere, the right people online saying something very important is coming. Then, when the records go on the radio, it's like a match to kerosene—there's so much enthusiasm it explodes immediately."

By the end of June, she was making weekly, on-the-fly short films documenting her life on the road; she called the project *Transmission Gagavision* and uploaded them to her site. She kept up her MySpace page and Facebook wall. She cracked a code that's ever-changing, specific to each person who tries: How to cut through the clutter of the Web and create an online presence that's not just startling but that sticks, that keeps people coming back in ever-greater numbers, and that then translates into the real world, generating actual currency—be they votes for president or tickets to your rock show.

"With the Internet, everybody gets distribution, everybody gets eyeballed," says MTV's DiSanto. "But fame and stickiness? That depends on the content." He points to the network's most phenomenal success to date, the reality TV series *Jersey Shore*.

"That was the fastest success rate we've ever seen," he says. "After Episode One, it's on *SNL*'s 'Weekend Update.' And people said, 'Oh, it's probably because of the controversy. Snooki"—the sozzled, Smurf-like guidette—"got punched and it's all over the Internet.' That's gonna draw people, but the stickiness of the show and the content is what made people stay with it. In terms of [Gaga], there are a million artists and a million kids out there putting stuff up on YouTube every day, so it's a lot easier to get seen, but it's much harder to get famous. Because with this much choice, things get lost in the middle."

DiSanto believes that the sheer volume of content that lives online demands that any emerging artist has to "go broad right off the bat" by, counterintuitive as it sounds, "super-serving a niche. If you're making a feature film, a giant director like a J. J. Abrams or a James Cameron will go to Comic-Con [America's biggest annual comic book convention] and super-serve those niche fans and get them to come along with you. Then you use your niche to be your root and blow up from there. I think she did a brilliant job of super-serving her niche, the gay fan base. You know, Logo [the gay-themed cable channel] was her first official TV appearance. She allowed that to be a real die-hard solid fan base that allowed her to go broad."

That first TV appearance on Logo was a performance of "Just Dance" during the channel's NewNowNext Awards in May 2008. "Interscope was really pushing this girl," says Logo's Dave Mace, senior vice president of programming. He and his team didn't know all that much about her. "She had the one video out, for 'Just Dance,'" he says. Though it wasn't getting much radio airplay, the clip was playing on Logo's video countdown show. "At that point, we didn't know if it was going to have any life beyond that, if it was a one-hit-wonder situation," he says. "But we really liked her, and we felt it had the potential to be a hit song." And she'd spent the better part of the year building a gay fan base. So they booked her.

"It was interesting when she came in to rehearse," says Mace. "She was mysterious and in character, with the blond hair and the sunglasses and the cape over her head. And then, like, no pants. When she walked in, you were like, 'Who is this girl? Who does she think she is?' But not in a bad way. Kind of, like . . . interesting. For somebody her age, you wouldn't expect that sort of thing. She reminded me of Grace Jones, that sort of mysteriousness."

Interscope, says Mace, "had clearly given her more money to work with than most developing artists. They'd been kind enough to pay for a bunch of dancers that Lady Gaga wanted with her," he says, "to kind of take over the room. And she had worked out this amazing choreographed number."

The performance was shot at MTV's studios, the same space where the now-defunct after-school countdown show *TRL* was broadcast. The space was retrofitted to look like a nightclub, to little effect. The production values were low, and the studio was small—so small that the bulk of the audience had to leave so she'd have room to perform; there were maybe fifteen people in the crowd.

As Gaga was introduced, the camera tracked her with her geometrically cut blond bangs and long hair; thick, angular black sunglasses; and cowl-like black hood drawn over her head, marching toward the stage with an unintentionally hilarious sense of purpose. She had two female backup dancers in tow, made up and dressed as to be barely noticeable, yet Gaga—in her tight leather pants, S&M chain belt, and aerodynamic shoulder pads—looked like she was leading a miniature army dedicated to the forcible spread of fabulousness.

Christian Siriano, the fashion designer and winner of the fourth season of *Project Runway,* met Gaga at the Logo taping; he was presenting an award. "I thought she was this weird little tranny," he says. "She had that persona, and she was wearing that hooded thing, and you're like, 'Who's this girl? She's a no-body. She needs to slow her roll.'"

He changed his mind after watching her perform. "She was amazing," Siriano says. They bonded at the after-party; she was very complimentary of Siriano, who was just finishing up on *Project Runway.*

"She said it was great to meet me; she was like, 'Oh, I'm such a fan,'" he recalls. "It was a total little love moment."

"The song was great, the number went amazingly well—but the rehearsal went better than the performance, and I think she was kind of disappointed," says Mace. "It was because her disco stick"—her illuminated wand, already a favorite prop and a reference to her lyric "I wanna take a ride on your disco stick"—"didn't light up when she wanted it to. If you go back and look at the video from the show, you'd probably notice it, that she's struggling a little bit." (It's unnoticeable.) "But she was a perfectionist," he continues. "She wanted to do it again, but, being an almost-live show, we couldn't."

Even before she asked for a do-over, Mace was struck by her level of commitment to the performance: When the song ended, she struck a pose onstage, gloved palms open on either side of her cheeks, elbows askew, face—what was visible of it—frozen, expressionless. And not just for a few seconds, for at least a minute—through the host's closing announcements, the thank-you for watching, the plug for one of her former compatriots: "We're done here, but the fun continues online at the aftershow, featuring Cazwell, performing his new song 'I Seen Beyoncé at Burger King!'" "Thank you so much for watching," the host's blond female sidekick drawls, languidly stretching an arm right in front of Gaga, who's so still she looks like she's turned into a biblical pillar of salt.

"Chris [Wiley, a Logo publicist] and I were just looking at each other, like, 'What is she doing?'" says Mace, laughing. "It speaks to her as a performer—she was in character, and she was very conscious of it. But it's just really funny."

She also appeared, very briefly, on an episode of the MTV reality soap *The Hills* in September 2008, performing at a launch party for a jeans line. According to fashion publicist and reality star Kelly Cutrone, she almost didn't get the gig: "I mean, it's L.A., it's one hundred degrees," she told MTV News. "But she's in this Alice Cooper [look]. I was like, 'I'm so not into it . . . this is way too Marilyn Manson for me.'" But the event's promoter overruled Cutrone; the word was that everyone at Interscope knew that this girl was going to be huge.

Gaga, meanwhile, was assiduously tracking how much radio airplay she was getting. It wasn't much, so after every show, from about two or three A.M. until seven A.M., she'd go into a recording booth and rerecord the intro to "Just Dance" for about twenty radio stations, specifically singing out each one's call letters until, finally, she'd recorded tailor-made singles for every radio outlet in the United States.

"She was very acutely aware of certain program directors," ex–tour manager David Ciemny says. "And if they didn't add the song, it was, 'What do we do?' She knew everyone at her label. If something wasn't happening, she'd say, 'Let me call that guy. What do I need to do? I'll show up at the station, I'll sing "Happy Birthday." I'll do whatever it takes.' Because it wasn't really happening in the States."

She was equally on top of her momentum in other countries. "Someone could say, 'Oh wow, 'Poker Face' is number one in ten countries across the board!' but it would be like, 'Well, we haven't been to Japan yet, they don't know who [I am]— let's go to Japan.' Or like, 'You're famous now, you're on the cover of *Rolling Stone*'—[she'd say], 'Well, I haven't been on the cover of *Cosmopolitan* yet.'" (She achieved that goal with *Cosmo*'s April 2010 issue. By the end of that month, she was on the cover of *Time* magazine, next to Bill Clinton, named number one among their list of most influential artists.)

In July 2008, FlyLife was lobbying to get Gaga booked for something called the Underwear Party, to be held in August at a gay resort on Fire Island. It was what it sounds like—gay men partying in their underwear. Daniel Nardicio, who'd originated the event back in 2003, remembers being surprised by the booking. "When she re-branded herself as Lady Gaga, her people came to me and said, 'We'd really love for you to work with her—she's hot, she's great.' And I was like, 'Wait—is this Stefani Germanotta?' She was great before, but she was a lot more Natalie Merchant–y."

Nardicio knew her from Michael T.'s Motherfucker parties and from "the scene," as he puts it, but he didn't pay her much mind back then. "She was cute," he says. "Brunette." But he didn't think she was special, and he didn't think this new incarnation, whatever it was, would fly. "She'd had this whiny, Long Island–y quality," he says. "There was nothing really super-spectacular about her."

Still, Nardicio knew something was going on with Gaga; FlyLife had given him a copy of her single, and he'd been playing it on his show on East Village Radio. "'Just Dance' was such a great record,'" he says. "That song really generated interest and heat. I had people write me, like, 'Who did that song?' and 'When's it available?'" He called FlyLife. "I said, 'You know what? I want to bring her to Fire Island and get a big audience and out-promote her.'"

FlyLife gave Nardicio a thousand copies of the single, which he put in every house he could on Fire Island. The week before the Underwear Party, Gaga had performed on *So You Think You Can Dance*. "Just Dance" was finally getting airplay on Top 40 radio, including New York's huge mainstream station Z100. Gaga had been crisscrossing Europe, playing small clubs, and on Perez Hilton's site she was now a recurring character, averaging a post a day. Suddenly, it seemed, she was breaking through the membrane of mainstream consciousness at a freakishly rapid pace. Nardicio panicked.

"I called her people and said, 'Look, I know she's going to cancel now. She's getting big, I know. I'm only paying her $500. Just cancel it now so I'm not standing there, day of, with my dick in my hand.' And they go, 'As far as we know, she's coming.'"

It was one of many very shrewd moves on her part—not only keeping her word, but keeping it with such good humor. It's also a testament to both her work ethic and ambition that she performed at the Fire Island gig the same day she got off a plane from Europe.

Nearly one thousand people turned up—equaling the number of CDs Nardicio had distributed on the Island. "A sea of gay guys in their underwear," as Nardicio puts it. "And she looks out in the audience at one point and is like, 'I am fucking *living* for you right now.' Because, I mean, they were really screaming for her. It was so exciting, as a promoter, because you get those moments where you knock the ball out of the park and you get the right person at the right time. I did that with Scissor Sisters, with Gaga, and of course, the Levi Johnston thing,

which is in a different area." (It's fitting, given Gaga's insistence that her existence is a meta-commentary on fame, that Nardicio would unironically equate the work he did for her with working as a handler for Sarah Palin's daughter's baby daddy, but there it is: Fame in America, circa 2010.) Gaga did three songs: "Just Dance," "LoveGame," and "Poker Face," had two female backup dancers, and spoke very little in between.

"It was very early-stages Madonna," Nardicio recalls, "like when she did *American Bandstand.* But it was professional; Gaga had been with Interscope for a while, so they brought logos to put behind her. They brought her imaging. But it was tight and bare-boned." He remembers being impressed that she sang live.

After the gig, Nardicio took Gaga and her entourage to dinner at a local seafood restaurant called Jumping Jack's. What he recalls of her look that night: wig, sunglasses, tights, shoulder pads. He did not acknowledge that he'd known her before, back when she was Stefani; nor did she. He noticed that she didn't drink at dinner. He thought about asking if he could "be part of this circus," but thought better of it. (At least at the time he thought that he thought better of it.) He liked her, but felt something was off.

"My first feeling about her was that she seemed a little bit entitled, a little bit of a privileged rich girl," he says. "And I realized that she is, a little bit. There's nothing wrong with that. But I felt like I wasn't sure if this whole Andy Warhol thing was a little too, like . . . I guess I was a little skeptical. I thought it was a little high-concept for a pop song about being drunk at a club and dancing."

What Nardicio missed—or what maybe wasn't yet readily apparent—was Gaga's sense of humor and her supreme self-awareness. She was a twenty-two-year-old girl who was smart enough to write about what she knew: cute boys and partying. As she said in 2008: "It might sound dumb because people like Bono are writing about world hunger. But I don't know about those things yet, so I write about what I know." It sounds like something Paris Hilton might say in earnest.

"She's since had money and support to build [her show] up into a thing, but at the time it wasn't very polished," says Nardicio. "And certainly her wig wasn't very polished. I mean, the girl was working on a budget. She looked a little more ratty, a little more raw."

This was nothing that Gaga herself was unaware of. In fact, before the dinner was over, she had charmed Nardicio into helping, for free, to promote her CD release party, slated for NYC's Highline Ballroom in October. And he was thrilled to be asked. "I said, 'I'm not doing this for money. I just want to be involved.' Because she's awesome."

In July, she performed at the San Francisco Gay Pride parade, wearing a black-and-white bodysuit, a new wave–style black tuxedo jacket (hooded, of course), and black sunglasses. The performance was tailored to her audience; one of her female backup dancers grabbed Gaga's crotch, and the disco stick featured prominently. She opened with "LoveGame," then went into "Beautiful, Dirty, Rich" and "Just Dance." The stage was bare-bones, audio cables visibly snaking along the lip, adorned with a couple of tacked-up Lady Gaga posters. But she performed like she was playing a sold-out arena; the performance was fully choreographed, and she elicited her biggest cheer when she said, "Being here makes me so fucking proud!" In what was becoming her hallmark act of intimacy, she removed her sunglasses for the rest of the set.

When, at another performance for MTV in Malta, organizers told her that her set would have to end at a very specific time, she flipped and demanded that her tour manager, Ciemny, fix it. "I gotta hand it to her, she pushed me," says Ciemny. "She said, 'Don't second-guess me. Just do it.'"

Her attitude took Ciemny a bit by surprise, though it was keeping in line with her demeanor when he'd interviewed with her just a couple of months before. He'd been brought in by someone on her manager's team. "She came in with her Ray-Bans and was wearing this Halle Berry–like catsuit and these really tall boots with stiletto heels, like six or seven feet high," he says. "All black. And a hoodie and a weave. She said, 'I'm very serious about what I'm doing.'"

After a five-day tryout, Ciemny was hired. He watched as staffer after staffer was let go; before the end of his tenure, in October 2009, he'd watch her (not really her, but someone she'd delegated) fire about 150 people in all. "Everything had to be perfect," he says. "If there was a technical error, she didn't understand it. On occasion she'd break down in tears after a show. Her thing is this: No one can do it as good as [she can]. She's very detail-oriented: 'Tell me why this happened; tell me why this won't happen again.' She was twenty-two."

Two weeks later, after San Francisco's Gay Pride Parade,

Gaga performed "Just Dance" at her biggest, most unlikely venue yet: the fifty-seventh annual Miss Universe Pageant in Vietnam. She got the gig because someone at the label knew the organizers and was able to get "Just Dance" played during the swimsuit competition. The show's hosts: Jerry Springer and former Spice Girl Mel B.

Gaga took the stage in the same costume she wore for the Logo awards, but her shoulder pads were at Tina Turner/*Mad Max Beyond Thunderdome* proportions—it was a new jacket, camel, with three-quarter-length sleeves. It softened up all the black PVC and the sharp cut of her platinum blond hair, bangs to the forehead, the rest stick-straight and long. Also, she was not wearing sunglasses: She wanted to make eye contact with the crowd and the camera. She not only had two backup dancers with her (again, in black bodysuits, plain except for the exaggerated shoulders), but she had the remaining fifteen Miss Universe contestants, in bikinis, dancing behind her, freestyle.

One stanza in, Jerry Springer announced, "We begin the swimsuit competition wiiiiithhhh . . . Venezuela!" Then Kosovo, Mexico, Vietnam—here Gaga struck her own pose, one arm out, head up—South Africa, Australia, Japan—Gaga remained immobile, unmoved—Dominican Republic. And then Gaga came back and took the stage for another stanza before she was interrupted by Italy, Colombia, Russia, Hungary, Czech Republic, USA, and Spain. Like Gaga, the entire thing was utterly ridiculous and secretly smart: Hardly anyone knew who she was, and she'd just gotten ten minutes of worldwide airtime for an extended remix of "Just Dance," to say nothing of however many hits the swimsuit competition would generate online.

And she got to break out her disco stick—which, by the way, she never let out of her sight. She wouldn't even check it with the rest of her baggage at the airport; she carried it on the plane, every time, and got stopped by security, every time. She really didn't mind.

EIGHT

THE FAME

*T*he *Fame* was released on August 19, 2008, to largely good reviews. *Entertainment Weekly* gave it a B-, noting that "in this economy . . . her high-times escapism has its charms," and even her future nemesis at the UK's *Guardian,* Alexis Petridis, wrote "virtually everything sounds like another hit single." "The full-length *The Fame,*" said *Billboard,* "proves she's more than one hit and a bag of stage tricks."

Gaga spent the summer and fall in buses and on planes, flying coach, crisscrossing the United States, poaching the full-sized pillow from every hotel room she stayed in for a more comfortable ride to the next stop. (Ciemny would always offer to pay for it; sometimes the hotels would let her take it as a gift.) Her schedule was crushing: up at seven A.M. at the latest, out doing promotion at radio stations all day, lunches and dinners with record company reps, playing clubs at night, back to the hotel, up early again, right on the next flight to the next town, straight off the plane to another radio station . . . wash, rinse, repeat. This went on for six months straight, with Gaga sometimes getting four hours of sleep a night if lucky.

She was playing at hip-hop spots, Top 40 clubs, gay parties, and shit-kicker cowboy hangouts—doing the same three songs: "Just Dance," "Beautiful, Dirty, Rich," and "LoveGame." She also played the kinds of venues familiar to most baby bands but always left off the résumé: amusement parks and high schools. She never complained, would never so much as suggest that any of these gigs were beneath her, not cool enough for such an avant-garde show.

David Ciemny called his wife, Angela, to a gig in Southern California to meet Gaga.

Angela recalls being surprised by the venue: "I was like, 'Oh my gosh, she's performing at Raging Waters?' Because it's, like, a bunch of water slides and kids."

Gaga took the stage at three in the afternoon, in patent leather stiletto boots and a black catsuit. It was about 102 degrees. The crowd was unsure what to make of her. "People were laughing, going, like, 'What is this girl doing? What the heck?'" Angela thought she was great.

"I went backstage with David," she says, "and he's introducing me to her, and as I'm talking to her she starts taking off this catsuit right in front of me. And I'm like, 'Don't you have anything else to perform in that's not so hot?' And she's like, 'No, this is the look. It doesn't matter to me how hot it is.'"

In October 2008, Gaga was booked as the opening act for the New Kids on the Block tour. "I'll take zero credit for her success," says New Kids manager Jared Paul, who says he invited her to be on the tour but was most likely told by Interscope that it was happening no matter what he thought.

"I remember sitting with my staff at a meeting and saying,

'We have no interest in this girl, but she's going to be a big star,'" he says. "It was pretty obvious the label was developing her, so it was a win-win for everyone." (As with most people, Paul remembers what she was wearing when they first met. "It was August, a hundred degrees," he says, "and she had a head-dress on and gloves that went up to her elbows and was kinda like, 'Hi, I'm Gaga.'" His immediate reaction, he says: "What's up with that?")

Again, Gaga was just happy to be there. But she also had a very specific vision for the kind of show she wanted to put on, and it involved several LED screens that would scroll "moving video," or what she called *The Crevette Films,* or *The Candy Warhol Films*—raw, creepy little shorts with expert product placement (which she would later elevate to a near art form in her "Telephone" video). They were unusual for an unknown artist playing to such mainstream crowds, but it was their very oddness—who is this blond girl combing her hair and staring at the camera and talking about God knows what?—that got the crowd's attention. Gaga shot these initial installments on her few days off, on the fly, in a warehouse in L.A.

The idea for the short films actually came from Ray Wood-bury, who she hired as her creative director for the New Kids tour. He took his first meeting with her at a small dance studio in North Hollywood. "She wasn't costumed or anything," he says. "We took a few minutes to shoot the shit. I had come up with this concept of the moving video, where you could pull it apart and piece it together and it sort of came together as her backdrop. It was totally a new idea for anyone who was an open-ing act. We showed it to her and she loved it and understood it;

the guy who was doing content with me, it was a good mix. She made herself very available; she took time out to videotape stuff in a warehouse just to get it on screen. Everything was hitting on all cylinders."

Gaga also had her disco stick and a special pair of video-vision shades—huge black sunglasses that played her videos. She hired a NASA engineer to build both at a cost of $15,000 each. (She also had a sunglasses fetish, and traveled with a case of 150 vintage pairs.) These sunglasses were dreamed up by the "Haus of Gaga," which Gaga has compared to Andy Warhol's Factory and about which she will reveal little: when it was founded, who, aside from stylist Matt Williams, the key members are. She will say that everyone who works for her in any capacity is a member, and that the Haus is all about helping to conceive and execute her creative vision.

Aside from dumping all her advance money into her wardrobe and show budget, Gaga would play club dates after each New Kids gig to earn extra income to fund ever more gadgetry, even though Interscope had given her more leeway than most developing artists. Her budget, Woodbury says, "was more than normal" for an opening act. "But I think they said, 'We definitely got a hit here; there's no reason to fuck around.'"

Gaga was signed to what is known as a "360 deal." In the wake of the hit the record industry took from both the digitization of music and the recession, labels began pushing these contracts. In short, an artist gets a heavier investment from a label than under a traditional record deal (thereby having a higher chance of making it). The label, however, gets a cut of the artist's profit from *everything*—licensing, downloads, endorsements, T-shirt sales. Gaga's deal with Polaroid, M·A·C, and any other company? The label gets a cut.

"When Interscope finally determined they should go for it [with Lady Gaga], they committed to spending a lot of money," says an unnamed source. He says that he heard someone ask an executive at Universal, Interscope's parent company, "How'd you guys break Lady Gaga?" And the executive said, "We threw the building at it."

"They did a lot of things to get her exposure," the source says. "They attached her video to other people's videos on YouTube so it came up automatically. She's one of those overnight sensations that didn't really happen overnight. A lot of hard work and long hours went into it."

Such deals, though, are a catch-22: Without the investment, the artists have less chance of success, but with the amount of money the label can recoup *plus* the cuts they take, the artists can find themselves barely breaking even, or broke. The kicker: Just 20 percent of an artist's product typically generates 80 percent of the profit.

Courtney Love Does the Math.

"This girl [Gaga] has been spending money at a multi-platinum level," says one high-level music-business source. "When you see a Gwen [Stefani] or a Fergie walk the red carpet, you say, 'Wow, they're superstars.' This girl came out of the chute like that. Her costuming is expensive—we're talking $100,000 an appearance, and that's without the band."

The cost of her 2010 worldwide arena tour, estimates this source, is likely in the range of $800,000 a week. "Every one of her revenue sources is paying for that," he says. "And I guarantee you [the label] is tacking this onto her publishing sales, her merchandise sales, everything. Guarantee you."

This source, as did others, predicted that Gaga would eventually be able to leverage a new deal, one more financially advantageous to herself, and on May 1, reports broke that she and her manager Troy Carter were planning to renegotiate her contract with Interscope before her second album's release.

"I think [the label] realizes they're playing with her money at the moment," the source says, "so they could care less if she blows it."

"I know she's running into some issues on the amount of money she's spending on the road," says another industry veteran. "She's [got] Roy Bennett, one of the top designers—he's worked with Madonna, Nine Inch Nails. She really wants to make the experience mind-blowing; she wants people to walk out of the arena and say, 'There's nobody like Gaga.' You've got to applaud her for that, [though] it may not be the most fiscally responsible thing in the world."

Gaga, on the other hand, has thought, from the beginning, that it was riskier not to spend the money. Back in 2008, she said she knew exactly what she was doing: "People frown upon the major label system," she said. "I, on the other hand, am using it to my advantage. I want to create something huge and amazing, and I want to resuscitate the music industry, bring back the true superstar, the true artist. I want to create the super-fan again. I want my website to be Perez Hilton, but for Lady Gaga. I want people to feel part of this lifestyle."

Her willingness to spend freely—on set design, short films, costumes, stylists, makeup artists, dancers, business- and first-class tickets for herself—has caused, according to a source, fights between her and her father, who is her fifty-fifty business partner in Mermaid Music. This arrangement, too, is highly unusual.

"I've never seen anything quite like that," says Adam Ritholz, the entertainment lawyer who represented 'N Sync in their suit against former manager Lou Pearlman, which was settled in 1999. "I'm not saying it doesn't exist, [but] I have not come across a situation where a parent takes 50 percent of a child's income." Ritholz says that the parent of a minor who is in the entertainment industry will take a 15–20 percent cut if he or she is working as that child's manager.

"I have seen one scenario where a father financed the setup of a business for his artist/child. That's a situation where the parent invested very, very significant amounts of money and hired professionals and had a marketing and promotional staff and the whole thing." In Gaga's scenario, "there would have to be something that's not apparent to me going on here to justify giving half her income to her father," Ritholz says. "But I will tell you: If I was representing her, I think I would have a problem with that."

Her label, meanwhile, made her a top priority, due in no small part to her insanely strong work ethic. "Her commitment to her performance was really what did it," Woodbury says.

"We all did stuff above and beyond the financial aspect of it because you had an artist who was willing to do it, who was willing to get her hands dirty. When you have this really confident approach, very much 'This is who I am, this is what I'm about, I'm going to be number one'—everything came together."

She was careful to cater to the New Kids' demographic, domesticated thirty-something women on a nostalgia trip. Before the show, says Ciemny, she'd say, "'We're gonna give these bitches something to dance to!'" He says it was done with affection on Gaga's part, with the realization that a lot of these women were probably married with children and on a rare night out.

Gaga's elaborate, extravagant vision did not go over well with the New Kids or their camp, even though she had a good relationship with New Kid Donnie Wahlberg; she had cowritten a couple of songs for their album *The Block* and done a duet with Wahlberg. "The New Kids, they're pretty nice, but they were like, 'You guys are an opening act. This is too much,'" says a source who was there. "It's, like, 'Sorry, this is our show.'"

And this did not go over well with Gaga. "She literally would say, 'Go back and make this happen,'" says Ciemny. "And they'd say, 'You have eight feet of stage to work with. [You] can't do the screens tonight,' or something. And she wouldn't be able to handle it."

"She wanted to have a bigger presence onstage than what was enabled through the production," Woodbury says. "She kind of pushed some things a little too far; she didn't take no for an answer too easy. If you can take no for an answer with an understanding . . . maybe that's a bit of the blurry line there."

With the exception of Donnie, the rest of the New Kids didn't fraternize with Gaga. Every night, she'd ask if she could perform one of the songs she'd written for the band with them, and every night she'd get the word: "Yes, just wait in the wings and they'll call you onstage." That wound up happening only once.

"I'd have her on the side of the stage, ready to go with her monitors and her microphones on, and she's ready to do it, and then it's like, 'Oh, I guess it's not happening tonight,'" says Ciemny. "And I'd say to the New Kids' manager, 'What's going on? We could've been sleeping right now instead of staying two hours later than we had to.' And they'd just be like, 'You know what? It's up to them. We have no control.'"

Today, the New Kids' manager Jared Paul says, as do many, that it was clear Gaga was going to be a big star no matter what internal discord was preventing her from doing the kind of show she wanted. He sensed that, in addition to whatever the label was giving her, "this woman invested a lot of money, a lot of time, and a lot of resources into her career. This girl's playing to win. She was on top of things. And her manager Troy was right by her side and believed in her vision."

It took months for *The Fame* to chart in America. It debuted at number seventeen on the Billboard 200 on November 15,

2008. She was on tour with the New Kids through January, and the brutal schedule began to wear on her physically and mentally. "It got very tough," says David Ciemny. "Every couple of months it would catch up [to her] and we'd have to reset the dials." Sometimes she'd be forced to cancel a show, and she hated it.

"Poker Face," the album's second single, debuted on September 23, 2008. Gaga was steadily gaining traction in Europe and Australia, but her momentum in the States was still a lot slower. She shot the video for "Poker Face," which had a bigger budget than "Just Dance": She got to wear a gold prismatic face mask (which looked exactly like one worn first by Róisín Murphy), a metallic slash on her right cheek, a genius playing-card manicure, hair tied in a bow at the crown of her head. (The earliest known version of the hair bow was pioneered by the new wave group the B-52s in 1983, and was lifted by Karl Lagerfeld for his February 2010 Chanel runway show.) Gaga was also wearing no pants—a trend she set off for summer 2009—a cutout neon blue bodysuit, and heavy eyelashes. The plot involved her emerging from a swimming pool flanked by two Great Danes, playing a game of strip poker that devolves into an orgy . . . and that's about it. It took until April 2009 to hit number one on the Billboard Hot 100 singles chart in the U.S. By that time, she was huge in the UK.

She was also a lonely young woman who'd spent the better part of the year on the road with almost no days off. What

158

little downtime she had was spent in a tanning booth or watching monster movies or *Family Guy,* one of her favorite TV shows. She couldn't be on her own, not for a minute, not even to take a shower or a nap. The aversion to solitude witnessed by Wendy Starland eighteen months earlier had become exponentially worse. Gaga had recruited David Ciemny's wife, Angela, to work as her personal assistant, with the promise that she'd be "really nice" to work for. Angela says she was reluctant; she'd wanted David off the tour so she could conceive. Gaga convinced her: "She said, 'Angela, if you come on tour with me, I'll let you sleep with David so you can get pregnant.' And she would tell me, every night, 'OK, Ange, you and Dave can go in the back of the bus from ten o'clock to midnight.'"

In reality, says Angela, she wound up sleeping with Gaga more often than her own husband. She says there was nothing sexual about it; Gaga couldn't sleep without someone next to her in bed. Around the time Angela had been hired, Gaga and Matt Williams, who she'd begun dating not long after she'd hired him, had broken up, and he began dating another stylist, Erin Hirsh. Within months Hirsh was pregnant with Williams's baby, and Gaga would alternate between laughing it off or, in more vulnerable moments, confessing her hurt. She also still very much missed Lüc, thought about him and talked about him all the time. She was a young woman who'd grown up with parents who were always there for her, who had a very privileged, sheltered existence in Manhattan, who had friends who were at home being twenty-two, going to school and parties and hooking up with boys and nursing hangovers and cramming for finals. Average stuff. She didn't want to be average, but it was harder than she'd expected to be out on the road all the time, surrounded by a crew of people who were very nice to her but were nonetheless on the payroll. They weren't real friends.

She kept Williams on her team, though, and kept things as professional as possible, impressive for someone so adrift and who'd just lost one of her few confidants. At worst, she'd ask a member of her staff to act as an intermediary, to call Matt and relay a message.

For the most part, she struggled.

Angela tried to help. She says she assumed an "older sister" role with Gaga, and rhapsodizes about fifteen-minute trips to the tanning salon together as evidence of their bond. Whatever other downtime Gaga had was spent either monitoring her media coverage online or looking through the handmade notes and tributes fans had given her, which she carried in her hand-bag. "We literally . . . we would do our makeup together every morning and get ready for bed together at night," Angela says. They'd also take showers together, she says, because they'd have so little time to get out the door in the morning. But it was also, she says, a way to bond.

The few times Angela would start to go back to her and David's room at the end of a day, she says, Gaga would spi-ral. "I would say, 'Gaga, I have a husband to go home to. I'll be in the room next door.' And she'd call and text me: 'I miss you, Ange, can you come back?' And she would tell Dave, 'Can your wife please stay with me tonight?' [So] I would sleep in her room, because what's the point of going to my own room with David when I have to wake up in an hour and be here?"

How to reconcile this account of loneliness and neediness with the same fearless performer who declares herself "a free bitch!" show after show? "It's funny," says a source. "She's just always had this incredible strength, and yet, at the same time, she's very needy privately."

Somehow, Angela wound up getting pregnant on the road, and says that her relationship with Gaga and her manager, Troy Carter, began to suffer. "The second month, I started having morning sickness really bad and it put a strain, I think, on our relationship. I would say, 'I'm not going to do the five A.M. call, because I'm going to be throwing up, so I'll see you at eight A.M. instead. But I already have your bags packed.'" That would be okay until Gaga began prepping for her show later in the day. "It would not be good for her, because guess what, she'd get [to the venue] and start getting ready and she'd be like, 'Ange packed this stuff, and I don't know where anything is and I gotta be onstage in fifteen minutes and I can't find my eyelashes!' Or whatever."

Not long after, Angela forgot to pack fresh panty hose for a morning show appearance. She says she knew then that she had to quit, that this mistake was too big. "Troy just looks at me, like, 'Angela, are you kidding?' He said, 'She needs stockings without holes in them.' And I was like, 'I'm really sorry, it'll never happen again, you don't even need to tell me.'"

Not long after, Angela told Gaga that she was leaving.

THE FAME

161

♦ ♦ ♦

Almost immediately after getting off the New Kids' tour,
Gaga embarked on the Pussycat Dolls' European tour as an
opener. The reaction among the Dolls and their staff was not unlike the attitude the New Kids and their manager had: in short,
confusion and disinterest.

"I believe it was Jimmy Iovine's idea," says Nicole Scherzinger,
lead singer of the Dolls. She is speaking by phone early one morning before heading to rehearsal for *Dancing with the Stars,*
where she is competing against, among others, reality TV vil-
lain Kate Gosselin and astronaut Buzz Aldrin.

"Keep in mind, Gaga wasn't . . . I think she might've had
one single out. 'Just Dance,'" says Scherzinger. "No one had
ever heard of her."

How was it presented to the group? "[The label] said, 'She's
going out on tour with you guys.' We said, 'She is?'" Scherzinger
still sounds stunned and confused. She'd met Gaga once before, at an Interscope party at the Foxtail club on Sunset Boulevard in L.A. in mid-2008. "It was an event," she says, meaning
Gaga's entrance, not the party. "I was in awe of what she was
wearing. There must have been forty pounds of hair on her
head. Lashes that weigh a ton, they're falling off and she's still
talking and blinking, working her choreography like she's in
Jazzercize class. She's this ball of energy, a real girl, a real
chick from—I don't know, is she from Long Island or something?"

New York City.

"She thinks fast, talks fast," says Scherzinger. "She was just dynamic."

In March, Lady Gaga began her own twenty-three-date headlining tour of the States, playing smaller venues like the House of Blues in Chicago and the 9:30 club in Washington, D.C. She called it "The Fame Ball," and while on the road with the Pussycat Dolls, she and the Haus had worked out three different versions of the show to fit the varying sizes and scopes of the venues. She vetted and hired every member of the road crew herself. "She said, 'I went to this rock show and it was one of the best I've ever seen,'" says David Ciemny, who can't recall the band but says "it was one of those acts from England that all look the same and have guitars." Anyway: "She said, 'I went to this show and I'll never forget the lighting. Find the guy who did that tour.'" So Ciemny tracked down the lighting designer—Martin Phillips, who'd designed the lighting for Nine Inch Nails and Daft Punk—and flew to meet with him in London, and hired him.

"Every show's gonna be an 'A' show by the time I'm done screaming at everyone, 'Hang it! Hang it! Find a place to hang it!'" Gaga told Billboard.com. "That's gonna be my motto."

As the tour was under way, "Just Dance" and "Poker Face" were in heavy rotation on the radio. If given two days off in a row, Gaga would take, at most, one, and spend the other either shooting new short films in a warehouse, or doing interviews, or brainstorming with Matt Williams about wardrobe, makeup, set design. Her look was becoming more sophisticated, although

she was constrained by her budget. Her weave, for example, was an unyielding nightmare.

"For the first year I worked for her, her hair was a really big issue," says David Ciemny. Gaga's staff would worry about where they'd get the next batch from (mostly India), whether it was the right blond, whether they could get her an appointment with one of the few people who knew how to do a weave right. "It was really tough for her," says a source. "When you have a weave, you can't wash your hair." Her scalp would get irritated, and she'd have to have the weave removed and replaced once every three weeks at a cost of $400–$700; it was a six-hour process that at times couldn't begin until two in the morning.

"It was so painful that she'd be crying," says the source. "It sounds silly, like she's such a tough person she was willing to endure the weave. But she is a slave to her image. It's what she lives for. So she endured."

She was finally freed of the weave in December 2008. She was at home in New York City, staying with her parents, booked to perform at the Jingle Ball at Madison Square Garden, put on every year by Z100, one of the biggest FM stations in the country. She was also headlining the New Year's Eve Ball at Webster Hall in the East Village (tickets started at $75; the club held 2,500 people). So the hair was important.

She got to the salon at six A.M. to have her weave removed, her hair dyed blond, again, and extensions put in. Angela Ciemny had flown in to see her perform, and she went with Gaga's mother, Cynthia, and her younger sister, Natali, to pick her up at noon.

That weave, Angela says, "was, like, the hardest, most horrendous thing ever. It was so hard, for her and for me." She says that, during the ride home from the salon, the relief felt by all was overwhelming. "All of us girls broke down in tears, just crying," she says. "We were just so excited for her. She was, like, running her fingers through her natural hair, which she hadn't touched in months. I'll never forget it."

Scherzinger, too, was struck by Gaga's dedication to her aesthetic. "I remember once, on tour, we're at the airport for a seven A.M. international flight, and she rolls through the airport in a pair of nude fishnets, a thong, a blazer not long enough to cover the thong, a bra, and the most ginormous heels ever. She lives Gaga. I think sometimes she sleeps in fishnets and heels."

Unless she had the tiniest window between sleep and a crushingly early flight, Gaga would dress like any other young girl on a lazy weekend: jeans, T-shirts, no makeup. She enjoyed the relative ease with which she could be anonymous. But once the tabloid press in England—where she was far more famous—started shooting her without makeup, she refused to risk being caught undone. "It became even more work for her," says Angela Ciemny.

In America, she got booked on *Jimmy Kimmel Live, The Tonight Show,* and *The View.* She had trouble ceding control, according to David Ciemny. "The only time she would really wig out and stress was before television," he says. After each taping, she'd ask to see the footage before it went to air. "She'd say, 'I want to talk to the director'—these thirty-year-veteran

Hollywood producers and directors who are making $500 a minute, and the director's like, 'Who are you?'" Ciemny says. It's an unusual request, but one that would almost always be granted.

She'd watch footage of her performance in much the same way athletes watch film of their game. "She'd say, 'Oh my gosh, was I pitchy there? Is that cool? Is it livable?'" he says. Doing it over, he says, was often not an option, but that didn't mean she wouldn't ask—just as she had done after her very first TV appearance, on the Logo awards. "You know what?" asks Ciemny. "Michael Jackson was the same way."

In December 2008, "Just Dance" was nominated for a Grammy. In February 2009 she performed at the Brit Awards, singing with the Pet Shop Boys, dressed as a teacup. By April 2009 she was a major star in the UK: Her album had hit number one and she was a tabloid favorite. She also started carrying a purple teacup and saucer with her everywhere, which she called performance art. The teacup, by dint of its association with her, became a media sensation: People wanted to know where it came from, why she was carrying it, and if she wasn't carrying it, why not?

"She hasn't got a name but she's quite famous now, so I made her stay in today," Gaga said at the time. She brought the cup along—and held it up in the camera frame for ten minutes straight—when she appeared on the BBC's popular talk show *Friday Night with Jonathan Ross*. The interview generated headlines in the wake of Ross asking her about rumors she was either a man or a hermaphrodite. (These were reignited after her appearance at the Glastonbury Festival a few weeks later.)

She was unfazed: "I have a really big donkey dick," she said, getting a huge laugh from the crowd. She juxtaposed her bravado with an imitation of Princess Diana, answering Ross's questions in little-girl upspeak, tilting her chin down and peeking up at him through her long bangs, as though looking for approval.

Gaga has often said that *The Fame* and *The Fame Monster* are in part inspired by Diana and her death, following a high-speed paparazzi chase, in a tunnel in Paris in August 1997. (She would later say that her groundbreaking MTV VMA performance later that year was a commentary on Diana's death, a loose association at best.) Her old friend the photographer Warwick Saint, who was with her that night in England, says Gaga actually loves being trailed by paparazzi. "We got into these minivans at the BBC and I look out the back window and there's all these motorbikes," he recalls. "And she just says, 'You ain't seen nothing yet, Warwick.' I think she likes it. It's her natural habitat; she takes to it like a fish to water. She would talk to her team in the car and be like, 'Just make sure I look good.'"

After dinner at a swank Chinese restaurant in Soho called Hakkasan, the entourage headed to the exclusive Groucho Club. It doesn't matter if what followed is true or not—that it made the papers and blogs was Gaga's point: She goes to dinner after the show, gets in her car, is driven back to the hotel, goes up to her room, and realizes she left her teacup at the restaurant, and sends a car back to pick it up.

The *Sun*—possibly Britain's trashiest tabloid—ran a dramatic account of this ridiculous pop star demand. The relevant portion:

A source said: "She kicked up a stink and demanded someone get her cup and saucer back.

"She wouldn't drink out of anything else. It just looked like any other cup and saucer to me and said 'Made in China' on the bottom. It seemed a lot of fuss over nothing."

A spokesman for Lady Gaga said: "Lady Gaga does not want to reveal anything about the teacup itself, but drinking ginger tea is very good for singers."

Saint, who wound up hanging with Gaga that night almost accidentally—he was so excited to receive a last-minute invitation from her to hang out that he pushed his departing flight back till the next morning—says the night was all "lychee martinis and great food. And she paid the bill. I haven't seen or spoken to her since."

Lady Gaga was still struggling to achieve anything near that level of recognition in the States. In March she was scheduled to appear on the morning talk show *The View*, which was broadcasting live from Disneyland. She had to be on location by five A.M. for the eight A.M. broadcast to the East Coast, where the show would air live at eleven A.M.

A few days before, journalist Jonah Weiner had interviewed her in L.A. She'd just come from an appearance at KIIS FM in Burbank, where Weiner had watched her perform live in the studio.

"We were supposed to meet in her apartment in Koreatown," Weiner says. He'd Google-mapped the address and discovered it was in a very generic, middle-class neighborhood, "tract houses and minivans," he says. Then her publicist switched the location to a concrete park for corporate-worker lunch breaks.

When they met, Gaga was wearing white latex pants, a lavender leather blazer with gloves sewn on the sleeves, and sunglasses shaped like a trapezoid. She told Weiner, "I kind of realized I didn't want you to see where I live." He suspected that she hadn't had much in the way of media training, which is basically an intense course in how to deal with interviews and publicity, to have a politic answer and talking points always at the ready, to deflect and defend.

"It seemed like she was trying to figure out, on the fly, the face she was going to put forward, how much of herself she was willing to give," he says. "This was her first major interview. It's that situation where you find your intimate complexity sublimated in a three-thousand-word article."

At the same time, Weiner says, Gaga seemed one pace ahead of him. When he tried to order a bottle of wine for the table, she declined, saying she was in rehearsal, but insisted that the waiter keep refilling his wineglass and telling him she knew how it worked, that journalists always try to get their subjects drunk, but that she'd be getting him drunk instead. "She was cultivating this disarming coquettishness, but always in big quotation marks," he says, "like a commentary on interviewee strategies and the journalist's interviewing tropes."

She flirted, but in such a way, he says, that she was almost acknowledging that the dual seductions in every interview resemble nothing so much as espionage-level attempts to extract information.

THE FAME

"She spoke in this feigned, almost little-girl voice, minding her p's and q's," Weiner says. "Which is a very useful juxtaposition when you have lyrics as raunchy as 'Poker Face.'" She was equally contradictory in conversation, seeming both transparent and tentative. When asked a question she didn't want to answer—and those mainly had to do with sex—she'd say, "I don't want to tell you that," or "That's nobody's business but my own."

The next day she appeared on *The View,* and her demeanor was markedly different from the arch hauteur she'd adopted for the UK: Here, she was the all-American girl who'd "hustled" from the time she was fourteen, who was just "so grateful," who would simply "say my prayers every night," and whose burgeoning success was "so exciting!" She was in an ash white bob with purple streaks and a white Judy Jetson–style minidress. "I am loving the panties," said cohost Sherri Shepherd. Gaga then performed "Just Dance" to a small crowd of boxy Midwesterners who bounced along awkwardly.

Weiner was at the taping and found himself summoned to her trailer by a functionary. "Someone came up to me and said, 'You are *soooo* lucky.' I said, 'Why?' She said, 'Gaga wants to show you something she's never shown anyone before.'" When he walked in, she was getting her makeup done, bangs off her face. She excitedly showed him a picture of a new piece for the stage that she was working on: a Lucite piano filled with clear bubbles.

"She said, 'Isn't that cool?' And I said, 'Yeah.' And I was dismissed."

The bubble-filled piano was a companion piece to the bubble dress she debuted on the opening night of her Fame Ball tour on March 12; she also wore it on the cover of *Rolling Stone*'s "Hot Issue" that May. It was a direct rip-off of a dress made by Hussein Chalayan for his spring 2007 collection—something she did not mention. In February 2010, when she debuted what she called "the living dress"—a long, architectural white gown, replete with a vertiginous headdress and expansive gossamer, fairy-godmother wings, that contracts and expands on its own—she did not repeat the mistake. In a tweet before the dress was unveiled at her show in Liverpool, she wrote, "2nite Haus of Gaga debuts 'the living dress' inspired by Hussein Chalayan, as a fashion moment to be performed in a 'pop show' at Monsterball."

Gaga's biggest break yet in America came in April, when she was booked to perform on the results show for *American Idol*. She actually pretaped her appearance, doing three different versions, and the setups and technical issues between takes took so long that, after the second performance, the crowd was told they could leave if they wanted; half of them did. An EW.com reporter who'd been at the taping described the audience's response to Gaga's first performance, which paired "Bad Romance" with the far inferior "Alejandro" and involved an enormous water fountain, pyro, dry ice, Gaga in a lace bodysuit over a bra and thong, and tango-ing male dancers:

"... The audience was left so silently agog by the spectacle that afterwards ... the PAs had to remind everyone that they were on camera, too, and should, you know, appear excited to be there."

THE FAME

May was a huge month. Gaga played her now-famous show at Terminal 5 in New York City, drawing Madonna and her daughter Lourdes, and suddenly commanding the attention of the industry. She played four more shows, one in Austin, Texas, and the rest in California, including a set at an annual lesbian gathering known as the "Dinah Shore Weekend" in Palm Springs.

"She wasn't a gigantic star when I approached her," says Mariah Hanson, who owns the venue known as Club Skirts, which presents the Dinah. But by the time Gaga performed at the event, "Poker Face" was climbing the charts, so Hanson was even more impressed when she saw how Gaga threw herself into it, "250 percent."

"She gave the audience—which was packed with gay men, which we don't usually get—so much love and appreciation." Also: She brought the bubble dress! "She joked around with her bisexuality, with the reasons behind writing the songs, and the audience just ate it up and became more effusive, and it just kind of fed on itself."

Hanson books lots of acts on the rise, and has often been underwhelmed: "For instance, we had Ke$ha this year," she says. "She doesn't have a great show. It's not like she won't eventually, but Lady Gaga was somehow born for this. She understands the importance of merging art and marketing. When we think of Lady Gaga, we think of Cher or Madonna, and she's been on our radar screens for less than a year."

On May 28, her epic video for "Paparazzi," directed by the gifted, idiosyncratic Jonas Åkerlund (Madonna, U2, the Smashing Pumpkins), was leaked. Or so she said on Twitter: "Stop leaking my motherfucking videos," she wrote. The controversy, of course, just generated more interest in the clip, a seven-minute-plus-long narrative in which Gaga plays a star who is thrown off a balcony by her boyfriend (played by *True Blood* star Alexander Skarsgård, who generated even more controversy with his alleged comments about his displeasure in having to kiss her). She's seen in a wheelchair, a neck brace, dancing, and making out with hair-metal boys on a couch, and then, finally, she kills her boyfriend.

She got a typically effusive assist from Perez Hilton, who posted it to his site with a review: "The new Princess of Pop, Lady Gaga, has created a masterpiece!" he wrote. "It is her strongest work to date. It is a mini-film. It is art. It is visual pornography. It is satire. It is commentary. It is brilliant! *And, we are NOT exaggerating.*"

It was her most sophisticated effort yet, a throwback to the lengthy, plot-driven mini-movies that acts like Michael Jackson, Madonna, and Guns 'N Roses produced in the eighties and nineties. Among the pop-culture references: Alfred Hitchcock's *Vertigo,* the hair-metal band Warrant, and Minnie Mouse, whom Gaga was dressed like in the murder scene. Her high styling was due to Åkerlund's wife, B. She built, among other things, the video's infamous tricked-out wheelchair. Gaga hired her.

"They hit it off, but she didn't last very long," says a source. Gaga mainly relied on Matt Williams. David and Angela Ciemny describe Gaga and Williams as "like two peas in a pod," both interpersonally and creatively. (The other key member of her team, and the only one whose tenure is as long, is her choreographer

Laurie Ann Gibson, whose most high-profile gig prior was working on P. Diddy's MTV show *Making the Band*.)

"Matt's not the most social person, but he's incredibly creative," says Angela Ciemny. "He's really passionate about vintage design in all aspects—technology, clothing, all that stuff." They research together, she says, sourcing rare design books and old biographies, then sketching out modernized adaptations, tweaking elements, working out logistics. Though she says "Gaga shared a lot with me about all the people in her life, and he's somebody that she really cares about," Angela admits that she knows absolutely nothing about Williams.

As with David Ciemny, Williams and Gaga were introduced by someone on Troy Carter's management team, and that individual will say nothing else. People who knew Williams in New York and worked with him in L.A. say they know almost nothing about him. He's from California. He wanted to work in fashion. He may or may not have interned at the design house Proenza Schouler. He rarely spoke. He disappeared one day and popped up in L.A., and began seriously dating Erin Hirsh, the stylist who worked for Kanye West. Hirsh had been approached by Lady Gaga to come work for her, but Hirsh had no interest. She recommended Matt Williams, who then dumped Hirsh and began dating Gaga. Williams told Gaga that Kanye was a fan, loved her style, and she'd get paranoid, warning Williams: "Don't tell Kanye what I'm doing!"

The one thing everyone does recall about Williams: He seemed to be an opportunist, and not a very subtle one.

"He really was handsome beyond belief," says one source who socialized with Williams in downtown New York in 2007, and who says that Williams was intent on breaking into his social circle, which included actors and designers and was led by Proenza Schouler's Jack McCollough.

According to one source, McCollough wanted nothing to do with Williams. He then wound up spending a lot of time with fashion designer Ben Cho, who was young, gifted, popular—the locus of the Lower East Side social scene. Cho was friends with downtown influencers in every subculture, connecting skate rats to starlets, starlets to photographers, photographers to artists and designers and musicians. He hung out with actresses Chloë Sevigny, Christina Ricci, and Natasha Lyonne; photographer Ryan McGinley and the late artist Dash Snow; singer-songwriter Chan Marshall (aka Cat Power). He'd give his friends tattoos, host them at his weekly Sunday-night Smiths-tribute party at a club called Sway. If you wanted to be in with the downtown art-scene A-list, Cho was the key.

"From the minute we met Matt, we did not trust him," says a friend of Cho's. "Ben was in love with Matt, and Matt hung out with Ben 24/7. We just thought there was something very untrustworthy and shady about him. Everyone thought he was a social climber."

"He was always so calculating," says another source. "I remember one night having dinner in the West Village with Matt and Ben. Ben was really enchanted with Matt, but it was, like, Matt was straight, of course. But he would always be sitting there [being] cute, and then he started talking and he was just kind of eager. . . . I don't remember it being Oscar Wilde in the garden, you know?"

"I remember Matt as young, eager," says another acquaintance from this time. "He was super fashion-y. He hung out with Ben forever and with [rising] photographer David Sherry. He definitely wanted to be connected to [the right] people, but I actually got a really good impression of him."

This source, along with Brendan Sullivan, recalls Williams's scene as mainly gay men who worked in fashion. When it came to men who were interested, this source says "he really wouldn't go there. He'd bring it close to that—sleepovers, shit like that—but nothing weird." One friend of Ben Cho's remembers Cho introducing Williams around as his boyfriend, and another isn't sure exactly what went on in that relationship. But Cho's friend says she believes Williams and Cho were a couple, and that Williams didn't care who he hurt, had no problem using people and tossing them aside when he was done.

Both sources say Cho was devastated when Williams suddenly picked up and left for California. No one knew why he was leaving or what he planned to do there, and then, months later, they heard he was working for Lady Gaga.

A knockout performance in a knockout dress at the Wiltern in L.A., March 2009.

Performing in her beloved bubble dress at her even more beloved bubble-filled piano at Philadelphia's Electric Factory, May 2009.

A Rubicon has been crossed: Gaga's bra explodes at the 2009 MuchMusic Video Awards in Canada.

The bow made of hair accents the architecture of the dress, and the eye makeup keys off the color palette: Lady Gaga toasts the crowd at Skylight Studios, NYC, December 2008.

Like a cross between a Roman bathhouse warrior and Tina Turner in *Mad Max: Beyond Thunderdome*: Gaga onstage at New York's Radio City Music Hall, January 2010.

Distinctly referencing another influence, androgynous shock-rock star Marilyn Manson, at the 52nd Annual Grammy Awards in L.A., January 2010.

Gaga at the opening of the European leg of her "Monster Ball" in Odyssey Arena, Dublin, 2010.

Part Sally Field as "The Flying Nun," part Madonna in her Church-baiting days: fishnets, nipple bandages, and a see-through habit make the standby nun costume thoroughly Gaga.

As a vaguely suicidal red-leather dominatrix with impressive abs: Gaga performing at Capital FM's Jingle Ball in London, 2009.

With fellow misfit Kermit the Frog at the MTV Video Music Awards at Radio City Music Hall, 2009.

In the stunning, ethereal "mechanical dress" that folded out and opened on its own, on Britain's *Friday Night with Jonathan Ross*, March 2010.

In full-on beleaguered star mode at the Marc Jacobs Spring 2010 show, New York City, September 2009.

The telephone hat must have seemed the only logical follow-up to the mechanical dress: Gaga after her performance on the same broadcast of *Friday Night with Jonathan Ross*, March 2010.

Working her skyscraper chic with her favorite accessory, her pink teacup, at the 52nd Annual Grammy Awards, January 2010.

A pearl-encrusted Gaga performs at amfAR's New York Gala at Cipriani 42nd Street to mark the beginning of Fashion Week, February 2010.

Channeling Charlotte Rampling in *The Night Porter*, a 1974 curio about a former concentration camp victim who, years later, falls in love with her Nazi tormentor. For some reason, fashion people love this movie.

NINE

OFFENDED ANATOMY

Back to May 2009 and back to L.A., where Gaga appeared on *The Ellen DeGeneres Show* in her now-famous rotating orbital headpiece. "It's my barrier," she told Ellen. "It's my Gaga barrier." Then she performed "Poker Face," starting it off as a lounge lizard/cabaret number before going into full-on dance mode, spheres spinning. The same day she had a shoot with *Rolling Stone* magazine from five-thirty P.M. to midnight, for the cover of their annual "Hot Issue," to be shot by famed photographer David LaChapelle, and then she had a live performance the next night, May 12, on *Dancing with the Stars*. The following night, she was on a plane to Australia to rejoin the Pussycat Dolls on tour. By now she was the only act on the bill anyone was talking about.

"We'd go into catering and there'd be the local papers and reviews, and the leads would say, 'Gaga dominated,'" says Ciemny. "And the Dolls were sitting right there. It was embarrassing."

Lead Pussycat Doll Scherzinger says she'd study Gaga from the side of the stage every night. "I remember watching her perform, her eyes," Scherzinger says. "I looked at her and said, 'I'm afraid of her.' As an artist, there are things I want to be fearless enough to communicate, but I limit myself sometimes.

She had no boundaries, no fear, and did it in such a creative, theatrical way, she inspired me to be like, 'Wow, you can do this.' She's got so many costumes, so many new ideas, the most amazing art creations on her head."

As for whether the other Dolls felt upstaged, as had been reported, Scherzinger says, "I don't think they felt that. I think they thought she was a force to be reckoned with."

"It was a little awkward," says David Ciemny. "There was a closed-door situation for a little bit."

At the time, Gaga had been dating a guy who went by the name Speedy (real name: Frank Lopera). She and Williams had broken up, and Williams had rekindled his relationship with Erin Hirsh. What exactly Speedy did for a living remained unclear: He's alternately been described as a male model, an artist, and an energy drink entrepreneur. He was mentioned in the *Rolling Stone* article as a supporting character, along with Lüc, whom she described as her great lost love: "I was his Sandy, and he was my Danny, and I just broke," she told the magazine. She also went on a bit about being bisexual, but how she didn't really want to go on about being bisexual because that would be exploitative.

The stuff about Lüc was telling; she'd broken up with him that past December, but anyone who was close to her knew she wasn't over him.

"I don't think she'll ever be over Lüc, you know?" says Angela Ciemny. David agrees: "She just has always had a thing for him that is beyond . . . and he knows it and he took advantage of it." Later that year, in November, Lüc showed up for Gaga's record release party at the now-defunct Virgin megastore in Manhattan's Union Square. "I would equate it to a drug," David says. "I mean, I talked to her for hours and hours about him. He came down to Virgin megastore and there's hundreds of kids all lined up, and all she could think about is 'Lüc's coming, oh my God, Lüc's coming.' No matter what she was doing, or what guy she was with, when she went to New York, she was pretty much going to be with Lüc."

He also showed up, long after their breakup, at her record release party at the Highline Ballroom in New York City, where, according to a source, he proceeded to talk about how she was lip-syncing too much and how he was trying to make her stop it. No one understood what she saw in this guy; as Brendan Sullivan puts it, "Lüc. Fucking Lüc."

Back to Speedy: "She seemed really gaga over him," says Scherzinger, seemingly unaware of the pun. "I remember her talking about going away on vacation with him." (The two were shot on the beach in Hawaii in June, and these were the first U.S. paparazzi shots of Lady Gaga, since she had become Lady Gaga, without any makeup on. She's wearing a black one-piece bathing suit and flip-flops; her eyebrows are dyed blond; and her real hair is damaged and coarse. Curiously, she seems to be aware of the photographers; in one shot, she's making direct eye contact with the camera.)

"Speedy was a friend of [photographer] David LaChapelle," says a source. "And David LaChapelle—Gaga put that guy on the highest pedestal ever, because of his art. Speedy . . . I don't know what that guy does. He would come out on the road and it was like, 'What are you working on?' and he'd be like, 'Uh . . .' The guy was all talk. But his thing was, he was really well-endowed. That's all she talked about. I would tell her, 'TMI' [too much information] all day long."

Amanda Lepore, the famous New York City transsexual icon and nightlife fixture, met Speedy and Gaga through her friend LaChapelle (she has been called his muse). She is also friendly with the rapper Cazwell, who produced parts of Lepore's first record (sample title: "My Hair Looks Fierce"). Actually, she says, she'd known Speedy from the nightlife scene since he was about fifteen and working as a club promoter at a gay night called Beige at downtown's Bowery Bar.

LaChapelle invited Lepore and Cazwell to his office in New York for his meeting with Gaga about concepts for her *Rolling Stone* shoot. Gaga then invited all of them to dinner at Speedy's parents' house in Queens.

"She was super-nice and down-to-earth," Lepore says. Gaga was still in that day's makeup, but was wearing leggings and flats. "She was talking about Lady Gaga in the third person, like, 'Oh, Gaga would do this,' 'Gaga that.' But not like it was her—like it was a third person. I think she's really crossed that boundary."

Gaga had also invited several of her old friends along, and Lepore remembers thinking how interesting it was that she wasn't running with a fabulous New York crowd: "They were very, like, *Jersey Shore*," she says, "with the fake tans . . . One of the boyfriends had, like, tweezed eyebrows and shaved body hair."

Most shocking, says Lepore, was that Gaga cooked dinner for the whole group: spaghetti. It surprised them all but was very much in keeping with the Catholic girl from the nice

Italian family on the Upper West Side, who says that a part of her really wants to find a nice man to marry and serve him dinner each night. When Angela and David Ciemny visited Gaga at her new home in L.A. in October 2009, she ushered them into the kitchen, where she was making dinner for Matt Williams; they'd been back together for nearly a year. She was in high heels, tight pants, and a black bra.

In Australia, Gaga's profile was rising; "LoveGame," released as a single there, had hit nineteen on the charts in April, and her video had been banned, in part because she wasn't wearing any pants. (What seemed outré back when the video was shot was, by the summer of 2009, a full-on urban trend; in New York City, girls took to wearing belted Oxford shirts, shoes, and nothing else—to work.) In mid-May Gaga appeared on the Australian talk show *Rove* wearing a simple white V-neck dress and an eighteen-inch pyramid of braided hair atop her head. She looked like one of the *SNL* Coneheads.

Her speaking voice had lost its New York outer-borough roughness; she was speaking in that higher, far more girlish pitch, regional accent buffed and puffed away, network news anchor–style. She had also begun to perfect the art of seeming remarkably humble while actually congratulating herself:

"Since we last had you on the show," says host Rove McManus, "you haven't stopped touring, and it's been nearly twelve months."

"It's been exactly twelve months, I think," Gaga replies.

"How's it all been for you?" Rove asks.

"It's been really amazing. I just am so grateful and I can't

believe it. I just played in New Zealand yesterday and"—she takes a breath—"twelve thousand people are singing my lyrics."

She also appeared on *Sunrise,* Australia's equivalent of *The Today Show,* and caught a lot of flak in the press for lip-synching. Ciemny says it was not unlike the disparagement suffered by Ashlee Simpson when she was caught lip-synching on *Saturday Night Live.*

"Australia does not, will not, tolerate track acts," he says. "It just won't do it." Gaga, he says, had played a gig the night before, gotten just three hours of rest, and woke up to almost no voice.

She was suffering from lack of sleep, perpetual jet lag, and a rigorous, self-imposed diet. "She'd say, 'I can't have that, I can't have that,'" David Ciemny says. "She always wanted salads, deli meat and cheese, and hummus and chicken—that was her big thing, hummus and grilled chicken. If she had something fried, she'd say, 'I totally splurged.'"

Like just about every other famous young girl, Gaga had to keep her weight at a ridiculously low level. "From the first time we met her and measured her and checked her for the final [ensembles], she'd lost twenty pounds," says a costumer who worked with her last year. "She self-proclaimed that she didn't eat for weeks to fit into the clothes."

Her schedule had, if possible, gotten more intense. Or maybe it just felt that way. Ciemny says that, during his time with her, he had to take her to the hospital at least half a dozen times in various countries; sometimes people would tell her she had to go, sometimes she would call from her room and say she needed to go.

"Her promotion schedule was ridiculous," says David Ciemny. "When I say she was sick, I mean physically and mentally. It was all exhaustion from lack of sleep, too many shows. There was this point of breaking down in tears, just so exhausted. The doctor would say, 'You need three days with nothing but sleep; cancel everything.' And we'd cancel everything. For twelve hours."

"She was just completely depleted," says David's wife Angela. "You know, I would call David and say, 'You need to call her manager and tell him she can't perform, or she can't get up at five in the morning.' And it would always be like, 'Ange, get her to do it. Get her to eat, get her to sleep right now, she doesn't need to take her makeup off, she doesn't need to shower.'" Angela thinks Gaga's only escape was the hospital: "I think these were times when it was, like, 'I can't be pushed. I need to check out.'"

The usual course of treatment, David says, was an IV bag filled with saline and electrolytes and a B-12 shot for energy. On those rare occasions that he called Gaga's parents to let them know their daughter was in the hospital, he'd catch it from her management.

"The parents would call the manager saying, 'Why are you letting there be a schedule like this for my daughter? Are you crazy? What are you thinking?' And then management would call me and say, 'What are you thinking? Why would you call the parents and make them all worried?'"

After the Pussycat Dolls tour, Gaga was off to Asia to do promotion from June 1 to 13; on June 26, she embarked on a two-month-long tour of Europe. In between, she went on that vacation she'd been telling Scherzinger about, with her boy-friend Speedy. They stayed at David LaChapelle's house. It was here that she finally heard back from Kanye West about an idea for the two to co-headline a tour later that year.

West flew down to Hawaii the next day, and LaChappelle photographed them for the tour, a Tarzan-and-Jane theme. "The whole Kanye tour . . . a lot of people [on her team] thought it was a bad idea," says David Ciemny. "Because Kanye's a disaster; he's just a mess. We all knew it was a train wreck waiting to happen. And actually it was Anthony Randall, her production guy, who basically said, 'Really, if you're doing Kanye, I'm out, I'm done.' She didn't care. Their relationship went downhill really quickly. He didn't last very long."

West and Gaga announced tour dates for their co-headlining "Fame Kills" tour on September 15, 2009. "I saw the concept book for it," says a Kanye source. "It was a really complicated, high-concept collaboration—it wasn't like, opening act/main act. It was this whole intricate, creative, never-before-seen kind of thing, with a lot of duets and a few new songs, this elaborate stage . . . it seemed intense, a lot for a new artist that's blowing up at that second to go off and do this other thing."

On October 1, the tour was canceled. The causal link was assumed to be West's hijacking of teenage newcomer Taylor Swift's VMA acceptance speech for Best Female Video, proclaiming that Beyoncé deserved it. But that, according to sources, was only part of it, and good timing for a classy bow out; he was public enemy number one, his record sales tanked, Donald Trump called for a Kanye boycott. . . . Gaga, meanwhile, was becoming increasingly famous, morphing from an object of curiosity and fascination to a star who was well liked in the industry and who was generating an increasingly rabid fan base.

"I know there was creative infighting before [they canceled the tour]; he told me that," says the Kanye source, adding that Gaga and West also had a "strained" personal relationship. "But someone else who'd worked with him told me that if it hadn't been the VMAs thing, it would've been something else, because he was just trying to get the whole thing shut down. It was just some fucked-up way of trying to get off the road."

"That turned out to be a good thing for her," says Gary Bongiovanni, editor in chief of the trade publication *Pollstar*. "You kind of got the sense that she was driving that tour; now she's going on, headlining, and she is the star of the show." (According to *Pollstar*, from October 8, 2008, through March 14, 2010, Lady Gaga grossed $12.8 million on tour.)

That summer, she was booked into two of England's biggest festivals: Glastonbury and T in the Park. Glastonbury was especially telling: Here she was, playing an outdoor festival in the daytime just two years after she'd had such a disastrous experience at Lollapalooza. She did five costume changes over an hour-long set, including a space-age disco minidress (a look she'd directly ripped off from Missing Persons' Dale Bozzio). She had three male dancers behind her. The choreography was tight; she had a new backing band; she was performing before a sea of people, fifty thousand in all, girls with lightning bolts painted over one eye in tribute to her.

Out in the crowd, a fan was wrapped in a head-to-toe pink body stocking; it looked like a human wrapped in a giant condom. Most everyone knew all the words, and she ended her performance of "LoveGame" with what would later become a midway punctuation point in her 2010 arena tour: She thrust her disco stick in the air and jumped up and down, and suddenly the crowd was doing the same, in perfect time. She also broke out her pyrotechnic bra, sparks shooting from her breasts, to the crowd's amazement and awe.

"Pop madness/brilliance from a performer at home in front of the huge crowds," said Will Dean in the *Guardian*.

"Wacky pop diva Lady Gaga wowed the crowd with a stage show like something you'd see in a glitzy arena rather than a dirty festival," said Nadia Mendoza in the *Sun*.

The *Daily Mail,* meanwhile, made note of how much Lily Allen—the Brit pop singer Gaga had once said she needed to "keep my eye on"—was dressed and made up like Gaga. Allen wore a shoulder-length platinum blond wig offstage and a lilac one on, along with generous half crescents of pink glitter under her eyes, a purple jumpsuit with a plunging neckline, and one white glove, in tribute to Michael Jackson, who'd died the day before, June 25.

"On our last rehearsal day, the day before Glastonbury, I heard [about Jackson's death], so I went over to where they were rehearsing and I was like, 'Gaga, Michael Jackson just died,'" David Ciemny recalls. "And she was like, 'Shut up, David, I don't even want to hear that. No. Don't tell me that. Don't even joke about it, like, seriously, shut up.'" So he left the room, and an hour later, she realized it was true.

"She was really shaken up," he says. She'd always loved

Michael Jackson, and, he says, "I think she had just found out that Michael was a fan."

She was also jarred by the rumors spreading on the Internet that she was a hermaphrodite, or a man. Video taken by a fan caught her at a weird angle, with her micro-skirt having ridden up and something fuzzy underneath, and that image whipped around online along with an alleged quote from Gaga on the subject: "It's not something I'm ashamed of; it's just not something I go around telling everyone."

She let the controversy and rumors swirl for weeks before addressing the issue, saying, "I'm not offended; my vagina is offended." (Speculation on blogs followed that Gaga was such a genius at generating publicity through controversy that she'd planned the whole hoax; sources close to her say that's not true.)

Gaga herself noted that the really important thing here was that she'd sold 4 million records in the span of six months, and she offered an astute theory as to why the rumor had gained traction: "The idea that we equate strength with men, and a penis is a symbol of male strength, you know—it is what it is."

TEN

MAKEOVER

She continued to tour Europe in July, and it was during this time that she met Nicola Formichetti, who was styling her for a shoot for *V* magazine, a niche, semi-outré American fashion book. The thirty-three-year-old Formichetti is half-Italian and half-Japanese and is roundly considered the most talented stylist of his generation. He's on the mastheads of *Vogue Hommes Japan, V, V Man, AnOther,* and *AnOther Man,* and is the creative director of the UK's *Dazed & Confused.* He's worked with designers and brands as disparate as Prada, Levi's, Missoni, H&M, Max Mara, and Alexander McQueen, whose work Gaga began to frequently reference and in some cases reproduce wholesale. These looks, however, read as homages rather than rip-offs; as talented as Williams was, and as brilliantly as he elevated her look, Formichetti is considered the true genius. Before Nicola, she could not get in with high-end designers; no one would loan her anything. He took her from a costume-y, gimmicky look to high-fashion eccentricity, and today designers fight for the honor of dressing her.

"[Nicola] is responsible for her hard-edge glamour look," says an industry source. "He definitely has an elegance or finesse that it sometimes seems she'd really be lacking, because she'd be wearing so many things at the same time, or the hair would just be so weird with the rest of the shit. I hear there are a lot of cooks in the kitchen over there. But he's done a good job with her. Her train-wreck look seems to be getting less . . . train-wreck. That's his influence."

The costumer who fitted Gaga for one of her tours agrees that, prior to Formicetti, there seemed to be no top-down decision-making regarding her aesthetic.

"It seemed like [her fame] exploded so fast that no one was really ready for it," says the source. "There was so much going on that it was hard for her—for it to seem like anyone was in control. It just seemed like, 'Make it happen, do the best you can, get it done.'"

At the *V* magazine shoot—like the early one she did with Warwick Saint in L.A.—her music was on the sound system. The call time was nine A.M., at Splashlight Studios in downtown New York; she'd just flown in from Canada and was wearing last night's makeup. Gaga asked for sushi, says an assistant who worked on that shoot, who recalls that as her only unusual request. "She hadn't slept and was still wearing her costume," says the assistant. "But she had a great, positive energy to her; she was open to everything."

The assistant, who was "convinced after seeing her that she was at least twenty-eight," was struck by Gaga's Donatella Versace look, which came off in the resulting photo spread as high-fashion (and prescient: she was months ahead of the *Jersey Shore* curve). Angela Ciemny says Gaga would vacillate between pallid white and deeply tan on a whim, spray-tanning one day and scrubbing off the next, with no thought to what it might do to her skin, using tanning beds when she couldn't afford to have fake tanner stain a costume. "It depended on the look she wanted," says Angela.

This look was not going over well with the fashion people on the *V* shoot. "She was severely spray-tanned," says the assistant. "She's really short and just, like, orange. She looked like a tiny Oompa-Loompa in a bodysuit."

Gaga kept her entourage in a back room, and the stylist doesn't recall seeing Williams on the set. Gaga and Nicola didn't really begin to talk until later in the day, and, according to the stylist, Gaga, in contrast to her usual, control-freak style, was very low-key.

Another source who was on the set that day recalls being struck by "the fake tan, really bad hair, and like, really cheesy style. She was three sizes bigger than she is now. But she was really nice. Behind closed doors, she's really normal."

This source—who also knows Matt Williams and Erin Hirsh, and is familiar with the back-and-forth relationships he's had with Hirsh and Gaga—says that Formichetti is solely responsible for transforming Gaga into a style icon.

When he was calling in clothes for the shoot, says the source, Formichetti didn't tell the designers who he was shooting—he knew that if he did, they'd send nothing over. Gaga knew, says the source: "She totally got it."

She was the cover of the fall 2009 issue, face chestnut brown, hair almost white blond, pink sunglasses on some covers, blue on others. The headline: "It's Lady Gaga's World . . . We're Just Living in It!"

After that shoot, Gaga hired Nicola—or, in her parlance, invited him to join the Haus. As she did on that first shoot, she continued to give Formichetti "a lot of leeway," says David Ciemny, who was also present that day. "When she really connects with a creative person, she gives them a lot of power." She was still insecure, and was vocal about feeling uncomfortable with her looks. After the shoot hit the stands and she found herself embraced by the world of high-fashion, she was impressed that Formichetti refused to accept clothes from designers who had been mean or dismissive about dressing her. "The thing about Nicola," says the source, "is that he's social, he's on the scene, but he's a very quiet person. He's very closed; he doesn't really open himself to a lot of people." Gaga's the same way, and they quickly identified each other as a fellow traveler.

They began exchanging ideas via phone and e-mail mostly, with Formichetti flying in for TV appearances or high-profile events. "Most stylists would say, head-to-toe, here's a look," says Ciemny. "But he gave her the tools. She would put the puzzle together from the pieces he'd give, and then add. She'd say, 'OK, I love all of this, but now let me take some bondage tape and put some Xs on my nipples and then we're good.'"

"As far as I know," says a designer who's worked with Gaga, "[her team] is Nicola and Matt. She does talk about everything being her idea, though."

She also wound up getting back together with Williams, who now had a baby son with his stylist girlfriend. There was, apparently, some overlap. "He went after [Gaga] big-time, hard," says a source, who views Williams as a bit of an opportunist. "He tried really, really hard, and he was around while she was with other guys. But why wouldn't he try to get her back? This girl is the biggest star in the world, he already had a relationship with her. . . . He'd be stupid [not to] want to go to the next level."

It's hard to identify the tipping point for Gaga, the point at which she went from being unknown to an entity in the ether to a celebrity to a superstar, but it's likely her performance of "Paparazzi" at the 2009 MTV Video Music Awards on September 13 was it. She showed up with Kermit the Frog, but left him in the limo, and sat with her dad during the ceremony. Hers was the first performance, which began as pop frippery, Gaga in white lying across the stage, an homage to Madonna's breakthrough performance of "Like a Virgin" at the VMAs in 1984. Halfway through she took to a white piano, dementedly shaking her bewigged head, one foot propped on the edge of the keys. There was a cutaway to P. Diddy in the audience; he looked confused. Then she was back center stage, suddenly dripping in blood, smearing it across her face, collapsing, obscured by her dancers, then lifted by rope above the stage, her pop-culture suicide for fame complete. She even managed to make the white of her right eye look like it was bleeding. That's commitment.

"The VMA performance was the big, total platter offering of Lady Gaga to the industry audience who might not have known her then," says MTV's Liz Gateley, who adds that it "confirmed" Gaga's star power. "Hers was the most memorable performance of the evening." She won Best New Artist. She'd designed herself to be the next day's headline, but she was thwarted: Kanye

West's onstage bullying of Taylor Swift was the main topic of conversation in the media and the blogosphere.

After that performance, though, Lady Gaga was a mainstream celebrity in the United States. In October, she received *Billboard* magazine's "Rising Star of 2009" Award. On October 4, she performed on *Saturday Night Live* and took part in an unfortunate skit involving a catfight with Madonna. Her musical performances on the show fared far better: "Gaga looked free and unrehearsed, and tossed off a rare medley worth watching," wrote Todd Martins on the *L.A. Times* music blog. "For once, it was nice to see a pop star stretching herself by doing something more than showing some skin and spinning around a pole."

"The thing I was most surprised by was her intelligence," says dancer Christina Grady, who worked with Gaga on *SNL* and other TV appearances. She recalls Gaga as being very in control and in command, and was there when she began playing around with the radically different version of "Bad Romance" she played on *SNL*, reimagined as a balladlike intro to a medley that included "Poker Face" but was mainly an ode to New York City.

"I watched her compose that in front of us, in a room of people with her band," Grady says. "She did it herself, off the top of her head. She instructed each band member which note to play on each part. She did it in about twenty minutes, max."

Days after her *SNL* appearance, she was a keynote speaker at the National Equality March in D.C. and performed at the Human Rights Campaign National Equality Dinner, where President Obama poked fun: "It's a privilege to be here tonight," he said, "to open for Lady Gaga." Also that month, she performed at the thirtieth anniversary bash at L.A.'s Museum of Contemporary Art. The artist Francesco Vezzoli created a portrait of Gaga in his trademark petit-point embroidery. Her dress was designed by Miuccia Prada, as were her dancers' costumes. Damien Hirst designed her piano; Frank Gehry, her hat. Brad Pitt and Angelina Jolie were there.

On November 23, she released *The Fame Monster,* which was basically a rerelease of *The Fame* with eight new tracks. The cover was shot by famed French designer Hedi Slimane, who has also designed album covers for Daft Punk and Phoenix but is most famous for his work at Dior from 2000 to 2007. *The Fame Monster* debuted at number five on the Billboard Hot 200 and went to number one in eight countries. "This becomes essential for anyone who even remotely likes pop," said Britain's *NME,* adding that "it's the moment Gaga cements herself as a star." *Spin* magazine's Josh Modell wrote that "Bad Romance" "plays like the best Madonna song in ages." *Rolling Stone* was a bit more restrained, calling the album "largely on point."

By now she was such a cultural force that even the self-righteously discriminating music site Pitchfork—which specializes in indie rock and alternative music—felt compelled to review the album. They gave it a rave, calling the first single, "Bad Romance," "arguably the best pop single and best pop video of 2009" and "template-breaking," comparing her to an artist working at the caliber of Madonna and Prince at their best and calling her "the only real pop star around."

She'd also exhumed the music video as narrative epic. The Åkerlund-directed video for "Bad Romance" was notable not just for its unabashed extravagance and dark humor but for the coda: There she is, propped up on a charred mattress next to a skeleton, staring into space and smoking a cigarette—which, in real life, she'll do once in a while—wearing a bra that's shooting sparks, the same one she deployed at Glastonbury. It's since become a staple of her live show.

For a girl who'd been accused by critics and peers of being little more than a cultural thief, she was suddenly the one being imitated. Fellow pop stars began copying the Gaga look, shamelessly and all at once: Fergie, Rihanna, future collaborator Beyoncé, Ke$ha, and, most notably, Christina Aguilera, who once cattily said of Lady Gaga, "I'm not sure if it is a man or a woman," and whose new look and sound and videos are, to put it politely, heavily influenced by Lady Gaga.

The girl who some stylists deemed tacky, unattractive, too short, unimaginative, and an otherwise blank creation of stylists became, suddenly, a gravitational force in fashion. At the shows in New York, Paris, London, and Milan in fall 2009, the aura of Lady Gaga was everywhere. (Givenchy's Riccardo Tisci was influenced as early as January 2009, when he sent a slew of bodysuits down the runway.) Derek Lam, a great American designer of reserve and quiet elegance, sent pants-less models down the runway. Michael Kors, he of the aspirational-yet-watered-down-Hyannisport look, used her music as the soundtrack to his show. Marc Jacobs's Fall 2009 after-party—the high point of New York Fashion Week—featured Gaga as a performer and guest of honor. In Paris, Gaultier referenced the no-pants look and sent a sculptural metallic bodysuit down the runway; there were the bows-of-hair at Chanel (Lagerfeld had previously referenced her rival Amy Winehouse in 2008, and uses her other rival, Lily Allen, in ads). McQueen's show—otherworldy even by his standards—was a Gaga-esque riot of cartoonish beauty, models tottering in the now-famous sequined "armadillo" shoes. (This was one of the head-to-toe McQueen looks she wore in the "Bad Romance" video.)

She modeled in a Grimm's Fairy Tales–themed spread in American *Vogue*'s December 2009 issue and appeared on the cover of the January 2010 edition of American *Elle*. The fashion trade publication *Women's Wear Daily* reported that, in the last quarter of 2009, expensive lingerie, especially corsets, was spiking in sales, a trend the industry credited to Lady Gaga. She told *People* magazine that one of her goals was to be the subject of an exhibit at the Metropolitan Museum of Art's Costume Institute.

In December, she performed for the Queen of England, suspended at least twenty feet above the stage, playing an elevated piano, gothic in its outsized splendor. She was wearing an Elizabethean-inspired red latex dress, eye sockets rimmed with red glitter. This, too, was how she presented herself to the queen. She was one of Barbara Walters's *10 Most Fascinating People of 2009,* and dressed, for the broadcast, like her eighty-year-old interlocutor, who did not seem to get the joke. By January, she was on *The Oprah Winfrey Show,* performing on a prefab set hilariously meant to evoke a filthy East Village street, eliciting unrestrained glee in the gay men and middle-aged housewives in the audience. (She'd canceled a show the night before, claiming exhaustion; her fans, now known the world over as "little monsters," didn't care.)

MAKEOVER

Perhaps most tellingly, Gaga has evoked incredibly nasty and public comments from her peers. In addition to the negative commentary from Christina Aguilera (whom Gaga shrewdly and publicly thanked for elevating her profile, and who has since backpedaled) and Grace Jones, rapper M.I.A. recently shared her thoughts on Lady Gaga.

"She's not progressive, but she's a good mimic," M.I.A. said. "She sounds more like me than I fucking do! . . . She's the industry's last stab at making itself important—saying, 'You need our money behind you, the endorsements, the stadiums.' Respect to her, she's keeping a hundred thousand people in work, but my belief is: Do It Yourself." (M.I.A. has a child with the son of Edgar Bronfman, Jr., C.E.O. of Warner Music Group.)

In May 2010, niche folk performer Joanna Newsom got a lot of press for offering her take on Lady Gaga: "I'm mystified by the laziness of people looking at how she presents herself, and somehow assuming that implies there's a high level of intelligence in the songwriting. Her approach to image is really interesting, but you listen to the music, and you just hear glow sticks. Smart outlets for musical journalism give her all this credit, like she's the new Madonna . . . I'm like, fair enough: She is the new Madonna, but Madonna's a dumb-ass!"

By early 2010, Lady Gaga had brought her threat to her ex to fruition: "You won't be able to order a cup of coffee at the fucking deli without seeing or hearing me." She was omnipresent. In January, she did a four-night, sold-out run at Radio City Music Hall. Among the celebrities in attendance: her idol Yoko Ono, Sting, Donald Trump, and Barbara Walters. The New York

Post ran a fashion spread of fans at the show dressed like Gaga. The *New York Times,* which had run a negative review of her hometown show at Terminal 5 just eight months before, gave her a rave:

"Her voice is strong enough to expose in a cappella singing, and she backed herself up with her own piano playing, sounding like a female Elton John when she belted out 'Speechless,' wearing a huge black-feather shawl," Jon Pareles wrote. As for her showmanship: "No one in pop is more audacious about headwear."

"This pulverizing visual feast overshadows but never entirely overpowers the songs themselves, lurid and luxurious arena-disco anthems," wrote the *Village Voice*'s Rob Harvilla, "delivered by Gaga in a surprisingly lithe, confident, booming voice."

In February, she opened the Grammys, dueting with Elton John. (In a pretelecast ceremony, "Poker Face" won for Best Dance Recording and *The Fame* won for Best Electronic/Dance Album.) Giorgio Armani dressed her; she wore, at different points, a lilac spherical gown with Swarovski-encrusted platforms, a green sequined space-alien bodysuit, and an architectural, Ice Capades–inspired minidress that flared in the back to expose her behind. The outfit was topped off with a silver hat that looked like a cross between a lightning bolt and a glacier. The telecast had its highest ratings in six years, and the conventional wisdom in the industry held that she was largely the reason. Then she headed off to England to launch her first arena tour, the Monster Ball.

♦ ♦ ♦

By the end of April, Lady Gaga was on *Time* magazine's list of the one hundred most influential people of 2010. "An artist's job is to take a snapshot—be it through words or sound, lyrics or song—that explains what it's like to be alive at that time," Cyndi Lauper wrote. "Lady Gaga's art captures the period we're in right now."

True as that may be—she is a kook, an extravagant, shiny distraction during a seemingly endless recession and two seemingly endless wars, who just wants to make you dance—she is also moving the culture ahead. Her 2010 arena tour, which she conceived as "a post-apocalyptic house party," doubles as the gayest nongay nightclub on the planet, the crowd waving glow sticks, sweaty, shaved male backup dancers wildly humping the air, the stage, whatever, and it's selling out around the world, attracting crowds of all ages. The whimsical pansexuality of her show feels both of and slightly ahead of the curve in an era where gay marriage has become a polarizing issue but the president still says he will repeal "Don't Ask, Don't Tell."

The April 2010 viral phenomenon that was U.S. soldiers in Afghanistan remaking the "Telephone" video spoke to that: a fully choreographed production, on a U.S. Army base, with male soldiers flipping each other, falling into each other's arms and line dancing half-naked in patched-together costumes, one soldier with a huge "LG" logo hanging from a rope around his neck, nearly obscuring his torso. All of this is underlined by the seriousness of purpose on display for a song that's about a girl telling her boyfriend to *stop calling her because she's in a nightclub.*

"She's tapping into the curiousness of the moment, in that we're fascinated by extremes," says Ann Powers, chief pop critic at the *L.A. Times.* "Ideas that once seemed on the edge are now in the center. The most popular film in America [was] *Avatar,* we're seeing hoarders on television, plastic surgery advertised everywhere in Middle America. We're really having a moment in which the freak is the central figure."

What may be most freakish and original about Lady Gaga: She is a famous person who actually seems to enjoy being famous. She takes care never to be photographed out of character, and really, it speaks to her work ethic. At a time when talentless civilians thrust themselves in front of TV cameras and then complain about blogs and gossip and paparazzi, here is a performer—ironically and perfectly, a former classmate of Paris Hilton's—who writes a song about wanting to be both pursuer of the paparazzi and pursued by them. Unlike Hilton and her ilk, she has rarely been photographed looking buzzed, does not play out her private life in the press, is never caught doing or saying anything she doesn't want to be. She is unashamed about having wanted fame and almost never appears to be burdened by it. She allows the public to believe that fame is as wonderful as they might imagine it to be. It's refreshing.

"The way she carries herself as a famous person is very cool," says MTV's Tony DiSanto. "She's the ultimate aspirational diva, and she plays that part to a T."

That said, she often talks about fame—or, to be exact "the fame"—as her overarching narrative, about having always been

famous even when she wasn't famous, about her own fame being a meta-commentary on fame itself. But it doesn't quite work; it all ultimately comes off as an attempt to elevate the desire to be famous into some kind of art. And if you say it's art, who's to say it's not, right? As she once said, she's "a fame con artist."

The only other person currently playing with the themes of art and celebrity and hucksterism and the willingness of the consumer to be hustled is the elusive British artist Banksy, who gained international notoriety in late 2006, when, in a collaboration with producer-performer Danger Mouse, he swapped out five hundred copies of Paris Hilton's debut CD with original music (sample tracks: "Why Am I Famous?" "What Am I For?") and cover art. He, too, made the 2010 list of *Time* magazine's 100 Most Influential People, described by his fellow street artist Shepard Fairey as epitomizing the art world: "the authentic intertwined with the absurd." Banksy, unlike Gaga, does not grant interviews (except for the 2010 documentary *Exit through the Gift Shop*) and has never shown his face.

One high-level music industry source—who thinks Lady Gaga's "fucking music is great"—points to her accessibility as her only misstep. "The one thing she's done horribly wrong— she shouldn't be doing interviews," he says. "That really lets the gas out of the balloon. If you could picture David Bowie in Ziggy Stardust garb going on *Oprah* . . . you just go, 'Eww! No! You're kinda scary!' I remember kids getting beat up in high school for having hair like that, [getting called] 'freak' and 'fag.' If I were managing her, I would say, 'We don't talk. You're bigger than life. You've created such a big reservoir for people's imagination—let people do that, don't deconstruct it for them.' Everything else, I think she's executed to perfection."

"She's an audiovisual artist the likes we haven't seen since the Madonna/Michael Jackson era in the early days of MTV," says another industry source. "Others have tried. Janet [Jackson] was interesting, but no one has been as successful at making her video premieres 'events.'" When images from her video for "Alejandro," directed by frequent Madonna collaborator Steven Klein, leaked online, with one of her legs seeming to be missing, the blogosphere whipped itself into hysterics over whether she'd actually amputated a limb.

"The other thing about Gaga," says this same industry source, "is that the twelve-year-old kid gets it and the eighty-year-old grandmother gets it."

"I like her, and I'm nearly sixty years old," wrote Toto Kubwa on the *Daily Mail*'s website, in response to an article about the "Telephone" video. Gaga has been the subject of a *New Yorker* cartoon and of a new comic book from Bluewater, the inaugural subject in their "Fame" series. There were rumors that Gaga fan and Olympic ice skater Johnny Weir would skate to her music during the competition; he didn't, but he hung a portrait of her in his room at the Olympic Village, telling the press, "She needs to be there watching over us, protecting us." A clip of Weir skating to "Poker Face" at an ice show in Japan in early 2010 has, as of this writing, generated nearly one million hits on YouTube.

In April 2010, the *New York Times* reported that teenagers in China stopped saying "Oh my God," in favor of "Oh my Lady Gaga." The opening title sequence of the HBO hipster-striver show *How to Make It in America* includes a picture of a twenty-something girl, LastNightsParty-style, making a "little monster" hand gesture—the crescent claw that's a universal sign for "I am a Lady Gaga fan." The champion Filipino boxer Manny Pacquiao hired a Lady Gaga impersonator for his last birthday party, which, in the Phillipines, is practically a national holiday. When Tamra Barney of Bravo TV's *Real Housewives of Orange County* announced this spring, on the air, that she was getting a divorce, she invoked Lady Gaga's mantra, exclaiming, "I'm a free bitch!" In April, the Philadelphia Phillies' mascot, dressed in a bastardized version of Gaga's red lace McQueen ensemble, danced to "Bad Romance" as the crowd hollered and laughed. After Madonna, Lady Gaga was the second artist to be the subject of a tribute episode of the Fox network's breakout hit *Glee.* She is a constant topic of conversation in high-fashion magazines and downmarket tabloids. She is a lead story somewhere at least once a day. She is a universal subject of fascination.

She is also, according to conventional wisdom in the industry, on track for a decades-long career. "If she didn't have the God-given talent, the whole shtick wouldn't have any legs," says this source, who adds that she needs, like her idols Madonna and Bowie, to reincarnate herself. "I don't want to make any comparisons, but there are certain artists—Ke$ha—who you look at, like, 'What do you do for an encore?' I think that's why you're seeing her standing next to people like Madonna, Elton John, Cyndi Lauper, who are all coming out to see her and [endorse] her. It's kind of the reverse of the Lil Wayne approach, where it's all current guys endorsing him. Here you're having the leaders of the old school, established superstars like Beyoncé, saying, 'I want to work with Lady Gaga.' That shows you where she's going to go next."

During the last week of January 2010, Gaga shot the video for "Telephone" with Beyoncé; Jonas Åkerlund, who'd done the "Bad Romance" and "Paparazzi" videos, also directed this one. The vision: a high-fashion mash-up of American film genres, from women-in-prison-sexploitation to grindhouse to whimsically homicidal set pieces lifted from Quentin Tarantino's *Pulp Fiction, Kill Bill: Vol. 1* (Tarantino loaned her the "Pussy Wagon" from that film), and a denouement swiped from *Thelma and Louise.* The plot: Gaga's thrown in jail; she gets a call from Beyoncé, who gets her out; the two take off on the open road, making lots of double entendres; they pull into a diner, where Gaga pretends to be a waitress and poisons everyone in the place, except Beyoncé. Then there's a dance number. She and Beyoncé, wanted by the police, engage in a high-speed chase before probably driving off a cliff.

With that video, Gaga made Beyoncé seem cooler than even marriage to Jay-Z could; here's one of the most wholesome, clean-living R&B superstars on the planet playing lover to Gaga's jailbird and a homicidal maniac herself. As importantly, Gaga is seen wearing a pair of sunglasses built out of smoking cigarettes. The glasses now have their own Facebook page.

Gaga also continued to make fun of the hermaphrodite

rumors that had never quite died down, having one prison guard say to another, after stripping Gaga down and throwing her in a cell, "I told you she didn't have a dick."

"It's her vision, pretty much," says a "Telephone" extra named Alektra Blue, who works as a porn star; Åkerlund put out a casting call through the adult-entertainment company Wicked Pictures. "She was basically co-directing it. She makes her own rules; she's very fierce. She was saying, 'OK, I want to do this, and I want to get this shot, and can we do it over again? Because I don't feel like I nailed it.' She was very ada-mant [about] getting the right shots."

"The way people were talking," says porn star Jessica Drake, another prison-scene extra, "[the concept] was largely hers, but Jonas was structuring it for her." Like Blue, Drake was struck by Gaga's attention to detail, staying on-set to monitor every shot, every setup, to make her opinions heard.

She has always been about control: During a 2008 inter-view with a journalist who wishes to remain unnamed, she gave direction, too: "I don't want to [come across] as too quirky or smart," Gaga said. It was OK to mention that "I've done a lot, [but] I don't want, 'prodigy at [age] seven.'"

"On the set," says Drake, "she had the most in control—I don't want to say commanding. . . ." She pauses. "She was very much a commanding presence, without being demanding or diva-like. She put every ounce of herself into making that video. She'll do something again and again and again. She gives until it hurts."

Alektra recalls Gaga asking for another take for a close-up in which she forgot to wear a chunky ring—a key piece that would show up later, when she opens it up and dumps the poison powder inside into diner food. (It's a reference to the scene in "Bad Romance" in which she kills her boyfriend the same way.)

"She takes her art very seriously," says Alektra, adding that she was bummed when Gaga, due to unforeseen time constraints, couldn't take part in the naked jailhouse shower scene. She's still not over it: "I was so excited," she says.

With "Telephone," Lady Gaga produced something profoundly silly yet deeply resonant. The video itself prompted debate about the viability of the medium—is there a future for the music video, or is Gaga's stuff an exception?—and whether the clip, with its mix of sex, murder, and unapologetic product placement, was shrewd or merely salacious.

Blogs and media outlets went crazy trying to divine all the products on display: Miracle Whip, Wonder bread, the Virgin cell phone, a Polaroid camera (she is also the new creative director of a specialty line for the company). The Chanel sunglasses, the HP laptop that also showed up in "Bad Romance," the Heartbeats by Gaga headphones, the dating website PlentyOfFish.com, the Honey Bun pastry she and Beyoncé share. And, of course, the Diet Coke cans that indelibly doubled as Gaga's hair curlers, a look she replicated for her walk through the airport in Sydney, Australia, two months later.

According to Adam Kluger, president of the Kluger Agency, who placed the PlentyOfFish site in "Telephone," product placement "has been going on forever, especially in lyrics. It dates back to the seventh-inning stretch: 'Buy me some peanuts and Cracker Jacks.'" (He founded his agency in 2006, after seeing a spike in the stock of Abercrombie & Fitch after it was prominently featured in the lyrics and video for LFO's "Summer Girls" and says he now does $60 million a year in business.)

Only Virgin Mobile, PlentyOfFish, and Miracle Whip paid for placement, Kluger says. Polaroid "was a favor," given that she's working with them; the Diet Coke curlers, "a personal tribute to someone in her past," he says. (Her mother used to curl her hair that way in the seventies.)

The Hewlett-Packard and Heartbeats placements were, according to an *Ad Age* report, "extensions of Gaga's marketing partnerships."

"The absolute worst stuff revolves around the Virgin phone," says Jeff Greenfield, branded entertainment expert at marketing firm 1st Approach. "I don't think anyone believes Lady Gaga uses a phone that looks like that. And you think about her fan base—they don't even speak on the phone." He thinks the deliberate close-up of the product itself pulls the viewer out of the flow of the video, makes them hyperaware that they are being pitched a product. "It really sucks, because the video is called 'Telephone' and they could have done [something] really smart."

Where it worked, and where the brands will see a spike in sales, Greenfield says, was "the scene where she's making sandwiches with Wonder bread and Miracle Whip. It's almost like she's an actor; every shot makes sense. It's very subtle. The key is to [integrate] the product and make it part of the scene."

Gaga, of course, put a more high-minded, artistic spin on it: She would later tell Ryan Seacrest that the scene in which she, wearing a see-through latex dress and nipple tape, makes the sandwich with Wonder Bread and Miracle Whip, exists to serve as a "commentary on kind of being overfed communication and advertisements and food in this country." She told E! Online—in her Madonna-style faux-British accent—that "Telephone" is really about "the idea that America's full of young people that are inundated with information and technology. . . . [It's] a commentary on the kind of country that we are."

Critics didn't really see it that way. "Gay Christmas," said EW.com's Tanner Stransky.

"Last night's unveiling of the video for 'Telephone' was an important event in gay bars and coffeeshops worldwide, one that finally brought together two long-contentious fashionable tribes: fans of Lady Gaga and fans of Beyoncé," said Interview.com.

Even her porn-star-veteran extras were wowed. "When she walked out of her trailer in the latex dress with the pasties and the thong, my jaw hit the floor," says porn star Drake. "On camera it actually looks a bit tamer than it did in person."

The "Telephone" video generated 17 million hits in its first four days online and went to number one around the world as tabloids in America and the UK ran ridiculous headlines and columns that can fairly be reduced to that evergreen of outrage: What about the children?

CNN reported that the clip was banned by MTV for being too explicit, which, noted Gawker, was deeply ironic: "MTV, through years of cultivation of reality programming that infested its schedule so deeply, barely even airs music videos anymore . . . yet still feels the need to issue a ban on one it deems too provocative. Even more ironic is the fact that the network is alienating probably the only artist out there who still actually cares about making a good music video." (MTV News later reported that the MTV network had not banned the video and in fact had premiered it on Friday, March 12.)

Gaga's management and label, however, premiered the video on the E! Network the night before, as E! gave them twenty minutes of airtime, and, as Troy Carter told *Ad Age,* aired the video unedited, "as it was intended to be shown."

"'Telephone' is a masterpiece," wrote EW.com's Stransky. "True, I found myself confused during most of the video. . . . [But] it goes without saying that no one in the past decade has done more for the music video genre than this lady."

"The 'Telephone' clip is a big-budget, pop masterwork from an artist clearly familiar with the discipline," wrote William Goodman at Spin.com. "[It's] a Whitman's sampler of pop nuggets."

"As Madonna and Michael Jackson were to MTV, Lady Gaga is to YouTube: the killer app," said *New York* magazine. "She, more than anyone, has made music videos relevant for the industry again, proving indisputably that they drive up record sales and concert receipts." Åkerlund, who had retired from directing music videos, agreed to come back for Gaga's visions. "All of this reminds me of the big days of MTV, when every job you did made an impression," Åkerlund says. "People would come up to me and say they saw my video. That didn't happen for years, but now it's happening again."

ELEVEN

BIG IN JAPAN

*I*n Osaka, Japan—where she was completely unknown just two years ago—Lady Gaga is playing to the sold-out Kobe World Kinen Hall arena, which, from the outside, could be mistaken for a very large redbrick elementary school; it sits amid office buildings on a freakishly clean, deathly quiet street. Rock shows in Japan start very early—sometimes six P.M., eight at the very latest—no alcohol is served, and all shows end by ten o'clock. Every single person in the audience stays within their circumscribed foot of space.

The crowd is as disparate as in Europe: middle-aged men and women, teenage boys and girls, little kids. Very few people in Japan speak English, yet when the lights go down and Gaga's first short film comes up on the white scrim and on the two video screens bookending the stage—here she is, rotating in slow motion, black-and-white, face obscured, the robotic mantra "I'm a free bitch, baby," echoing through the stadium, over and over—the crowd understands that, and erupts.

The show is, by now, a leaner, tighter production than it was when it kicked off in Manchester, but Gaga has truncated a lot of the dialogue, the "we're lost on the way to the Monster Ball" stuff. Yet the crowd stays with her, and when she sits down at the piano to do her mid-show balladry, and an American fan yells out "Stefani!" she expertly plays to the crowd, speaking as much with her expressions as her words:

"What? What'd you say?" She widens her eyes, looks around, slightly chagrined, unnerved, eliciting laughter.

"What do you eat?" yells the fan. It's such a weird exchange it almost seems scripted.

"I eat sushi," she says, deadpan. A pause before she mentions the national dish: "shabu shabu." She mimes flipping sushi with her hands; the crowd applauds, stops, is quiet, rapt, waiting to hear what she might say next, even though they can't quite comprehend it.

The Lady pauses. She turns serious. She is talking about her walk, a few days ago, through Tokyo's Narita Airport, where she was shot by paparazzi carrying her white Birkin bag (starting price: $6,500). She'd taken a black Magic Marker to it and written a message to her fans in pidgin Japanese. The translation, loosely: "I love small monster. Tokyo love."

Her eyes well up, her voice trembles. "I brought my favorite pocketbook and I wanted all my Japanese fans to sign it, so I could always have you with me," she says. "I really love fashion, but I don't love fashion more than my fans." She is not being ironic; she believes that this gesture is profound.

In fairness, so does the crowd. The cult of personality is undeniable and not a little shocking, not least because Lady Gaga, as smart and shrewd and witty as she is, seems to buy into it. Toward the end of every show, as she is offstage for her final costume change, her grave, prerecorded voice speaks this seemingly humble but actually self-aggrandizing message. She calls it "The Manifesto of the Little Monster":

> There is something heroic about the way my fans operate their cameras so precisely, so intricately and so proudly. Like Kings writing the history of their people, it is their prolific nature that both creates and procures what will later be perceived as the kingdom. So the real truth about Lady Gaga fans, my little monsters, lies in this sentiment: They are the Kings. They are the Queens. They write the history of the kingdom and I am something of a devoted Jester.

The beginning and the end of that thought are totally contradictory, but as she said upon learning that Elvis Presley had done a song called "Money Honey" first: Whatever. She goes on with another philosophically mangled thought:

> It is in the theory of perception that we have established our bond, or the lie I should say, for which we kill. We are nothing without our image. Without our projection. Without the spiritual hologram of who we perceive ourselves to be, or rather, to become, in the future.

It's funny—and not a little poignant—to think of this sentiment juxtaposed with the Lady Gaga who, one week later, was back in L.A., hanging out at the ridiculously exclusive Soho House, a club so top-heavy with celebrities that Jane Fonda once walked across the room to Madonna during lunch and felt compelled to introduce herself without bothering to remove her sunglasses.

On this Wednesday night at the Soho House, Lady Gaga was just another twenty-four-year-old girl who, as she said to a member of her group that night, was "trying to get my life together," who was drinking red wine and inhaling sliders and pizza and mac and cheese, making out with her boyfriend, blowing off steam.

She was not, however, fully off duty: "She was wearing a sheer black catsuit," says the source, "encrusted with, like, a zillion crystals and rhinestones and all of these bracelets and a black thong with, like, chains off it, and eight-inch platform shoes. A big blond bouffant with a veil over it." And, of course, she was causing a scene, sitting on a couch with her entourage, "frenching Matt the whole time, straddling him. . . . God, it was crazy," says the source. "But I have to say, *work it out*. You are the biggest pop star in the world."

In May, Gaga performed at the Costume Institute Gala at New York's Metropolitan Museum of Art. Chaired by *Vogue* editor in chief Anna Wintour, it's considered fashion's version of the Oscars. According to multiple reports, Gaga had a meltdown and refused to come out of her dressing room; it took none other than co-chair Oprah Winfrey to talk her down. Observers read her behavior as uncharacteristically erratic and intractable: She took the stage more than an hour late.

That month had been exceptionally grueling: She was on tour in Europe, but had flown back for a live performance on *American Idol*; she appeared listless, her voice weak. She did the Met Gala, went to MoMa with her friend, the artist Terence Koh, where she was shot waiting on line to sit with the performance artist Marina Abramović. Gaga then flew back to Europe for a week, then back to New York City for twenty-four hours, where she performed at Carnegie Hall for Sting's Rainforest Benefit. In the midst of all this, she was also writing and recording her second full-length album.

When she's back in New York, though, she takes every opportunity to be as normal as possible. She'll dress up, but usually not to extremes (her sister's June 2010 high-school graduation notwithstanding). "I remember once we went out after working," says a colleague who asked not to be named. "She's more toned down, way more street. We went to the old bars and stuff she used to hang out at, to see all these people in her past life. But still always wearing high heels." She revisited her past life after the Met Gala in May, as well. The next night, she went over to the Royalton Hotel in midtown Manhattan, where her friend Lady Starlight now DJs a rock 'n' roll party in the ski lodge–like lobby every Tuesday. She wore her hair down, red lipstick, a jacket, and a bra. Almost no one recognized her. Then she went down to St. Jerome's, where Lüc was bartending and hanging out with his new girlfriend. Gaga flirted with him anyway.

The reaction she elicits in Japan on this night in April is exceptionally rare: The crowd stays on its feet the entire two hours; they wave glow sticks with abandon; they bob up and down from the knees and pump their right arms in unison. This almost never happens here; the crowd usually sits, polite, silent, immobile.

"It's amazing, absolutely incredible," says Tom Daniel, a thirty-five-year-old American who's lived in Japan for years. "I've been to a lot of shows [here], and this is one of the liveliest.

I saw Madonna here three or four years ago, and everyone was sitting through the entire concert." (Madonna hates playing Japan and has famously called the crowds "Eskimos on ice.")

"They're responding to a physical sense," says a twenty-seven-year-old Australian ex-pat named Natasha Cordele, who has shown up tonight in a black business suit, her head wrapped in black lace, a "Bad Romance"–inspired black crown on her head. (She made it after work, in half an hour, spent about $50 on fabric.) Lady Gaga, she says, is so "expressive with her materials" that who she is to the Japanese transcends language.

It's a phenomenon made all the more compelling by the nation's struggle with individuality vs. comformity, tradition vs. modernity, with the increasing socioeconomic power of women. The latter, especially, causes existential anxiety, even among young women.

"In the past decade, feminization has made great strides worldwide," ran an editorial in the *Japan Times* the same week Lady Gaga was performing. "The situation is far from perfect, but many societies are now making much better use of the talents of the half of the population that happens to be female. One reason Japan is so far behind is that it is cut off from these global trends."

So you can see what a Lady Gaga might mean to young Japanese women.

"She's everything to us," says a twenty-nine-year-old super-fan who goes by the name Junko Monster. "We have nothing except for Gaga." She is standing outside Kobe Kinen Hall with her best friend, Megumi Monster, who is carrying, in her hand-bag, a laminated board filled with pictures of the girls and Lady Gaga. It goes with her everywhere.

"She said to us [that] we're precious," says Megumi Monster.

"You feel her music and her art and energy," says Junko Monster. "I can't explain it."

Two nights later, in Yokohama, Lady Gaga is needier than before. She does her TinkerBell routine, lying across the stage, talking about the way TinkerBell says she will die if you don't clap for her, and she's like TinkerBell. "SCREAM FOR ME!!!!!" she exclaims, and she seems to really need it. "Do you think I'm sexy?" is another favorite, and she will goad the crowd till she gets the response she wants.

What's clear is that—despite having presented herself in deliberate opposition to the traditional manufactured sex bomb of a pop star, a girl who would never trade on her sexuality for fame—she wants to be the beautiful star. She wears a bobbed blond wig, forties-Hollywood-starlet style, liquid black eye-liner, and hot pink lipstick. She is made up to be pretty, though she'll still put on a white fringed column with an attached headdress that makes her look like Cousin Itt.

Junko Monster and Megumi Monster are at this show, too. Junko is wearing Diet Coke cans in her hair. The other day, she and Megumi wound up taking the same bullet train from Osaka to Yokohama as Lady Gaga—a total coincidence, they say. They are vibrating; they are the girls that Gaga spoke about onstage, who presented her with yet another handmade tribute, who taught her a few key words in Japanese. "'Awesome' and 'fuck,'" Junko Monster says.

Next to them, after the show, is a boy named Yuki Yoshida. He is tall and twenty-two and is wearing his own homemade version, in black, of Lady Gaga's famous frothy, two-foot-tall white headpiece and eye mask. "Lady Gaga set me free," he says, shyly. "What she did—her fashion, performance . . . maybe I could be Lady Gaga. Maybe I could create something. Maybe I have something. To be inspired is important."

There is a twenty-something woman wearing cigarette glasses. There are gaggles of girls in hair bows, blond wigs, and black bodysuits, neon skirts and slashed stockings. They overtook the nearby train station at two in the afternoon, traveling in packs, to the great bemusement of the middle-aged ticket takers and the young families who are here to go electronics shopping in the mall upstairs. The exuberance with which the Japanese fan digests, deconstructs, and reconstructs a look is unrivaled. "I'm going to miss Japan," Lady Gaga said from the stage. "Everyone is so well dressed."

As has been said of Gaga herself, the genius of her show lies in its mix of radicalism and rote, meta and mainstream. Half of the show feels like the most innovative, challenging, arresting pop experience on the planet ever, and half of it feels utterly dated and cheesy, the wanton indulgences of the failed theater geek. There is fog and pyro and her keytar. There is a lead guitarist who looks exactly like Sergio!, the character Jon Hamm so recently did on *Saturday Night Live,* a shirtless, greased-up muscle freak in tight jeans, long black hair permed and pulled back in the oiliest half-ponytail ever, orgasmically playing and convinced that he's wanted by everyone in the room. And then there's the giant "Fame Monster," a huge stuffed dragon that's operated by visible stagehands, and the tree and the bench meant to be Central Park, and the fake subway car, and it all works. It's a genius juxtaposition.

What Gaga said about her stage show in 2007, as a baby artist with big ambition, is manifest in the tour she's spending millions of dollars on now: "My performance has developed," she said. "I'm trading in stripper shoes for Jimmy Choos, but the grit and the grind and the hairspray are still there. [It's] the couture version of my downtown performance. It's more fierce. I've been doing this for years, and fine-tuning it as I go."

That she has. It's the on-the-dot end of her show, seamlessy executed, tighter and stronger and even more visually impressive than what she had going on in her debut show in Manchester eight weeks ago. But there is always room for improvement.

"Good night, Japan!" she bellows. This time, it's not just her bra that explodes. It's her crotch, too.

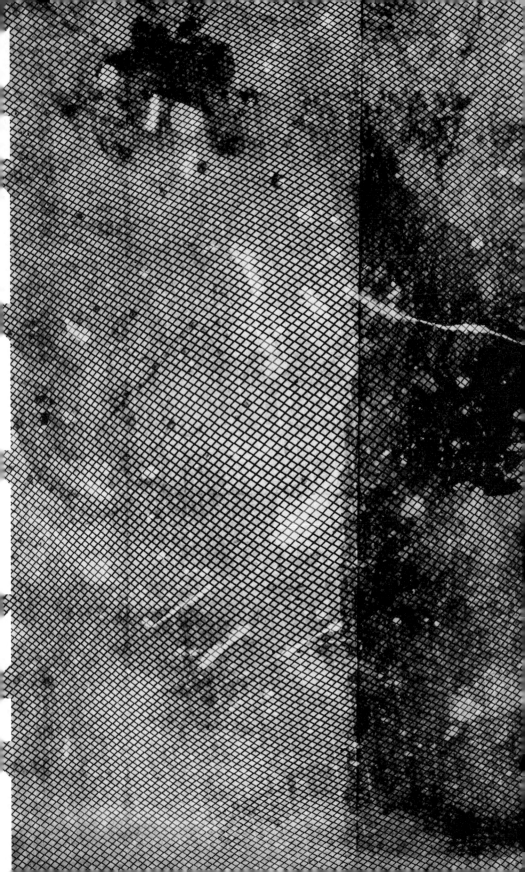

BIBLIOGRAPHY

ARTICLES

One

Callahan, Maureen, and Sara Stewart. "Who's That Lady?" *New York Post,* January 21, 2010.
Interscope press release, "The Fame," 2008.
Previously unpublished interview, 2008.

Two

"Who's That Lady?" *New York Post,* p. 84.
Barton, Laura. "I've Felt Famous My Whole Life." *Guardian,* January 21, 2009.
Previously unpublished interview, 2008.

Three

"Who's That Lady?" *New York Post,* p. 84.
Seabrook, John. "Transformer." *New Yorker,* February 1, 2010.

Four

Hattenstone, Simon. "Grace Jones: 'God I'm Scary. I'm Scaring Myself.'" *Guardian,* April 17, 2010.

Five

Love, Courtney. "Courtney Love Does the Math." Salon.com, June 14, 2000.

Vena, Jocelyn, with additional reporting by Sway Calloway. "Akon Calls Lady Gaga His 'Franchise Player.'" MTV.com, June 5, 2009.

Six

"Who's That Lady?" *New York Post,* p. 85.

Slomowicz, DJ Ron. "Interview with Lady Gaga." About.com, June 10, 2008.

Kaufman, Gil. "Lady Gaga/Rob Fusari Lawsuit: A Closer Look." MTV.com, March 19, 2010.

Seven

Thomas, Matt. "Going Gaga." Fabmagazine.com, December 24, 2008.

Eight

Graff, Gary. "Lady Gaga Ready to Go for Headlining Tour." Billboard.com, March 3, 2009.

Nine

Staff. "Aussie Shock Jocks Grill Gaga on Penis." News.ninemsn.au, September 4, 2009.

Ten

Parnes, Amie, and Kiki Ryan. "Obama, Lady Gaga Vie for Limelight." Politico.com, October 11, 2009.

Spines, Christine. "Lady Gaga Wants You." *Cosmpolitan,* April 2010.

Weiner, Juli. "This Is So On: M.I.A. vs. Lady Gaga." VanityFair.com, April 7, 2010.

Cady, Jennifer. "Lady Gaga on 'Telephone' and Its Hidden Meaning." Eonline.com, March 11, 2010.

Sale, Jennifer. "Johnny Weir Worships at the Altar of Lady Gaga." Examiner.com, February 15, 2010.

Corsello, Andrew. "The Biggest Little Man in the World." *GQ,*
April 2010.

Hampp, Andrew, and Emily Bryson York. "How Miracle Whip,
Plenty of Fish Tapped Lady Gaga's 'Telephone.'" AdAge.com,
March 13, 2010.

BOOKS

Herbert, Emily. *Lady Gaga: Queen of Pop.* London: John Blake
Publishing Ltd., 2010.

Phoenix, Helia. *Lady Gaga: "Just Dance" The Biography.*
London: Orion Books, 2010.

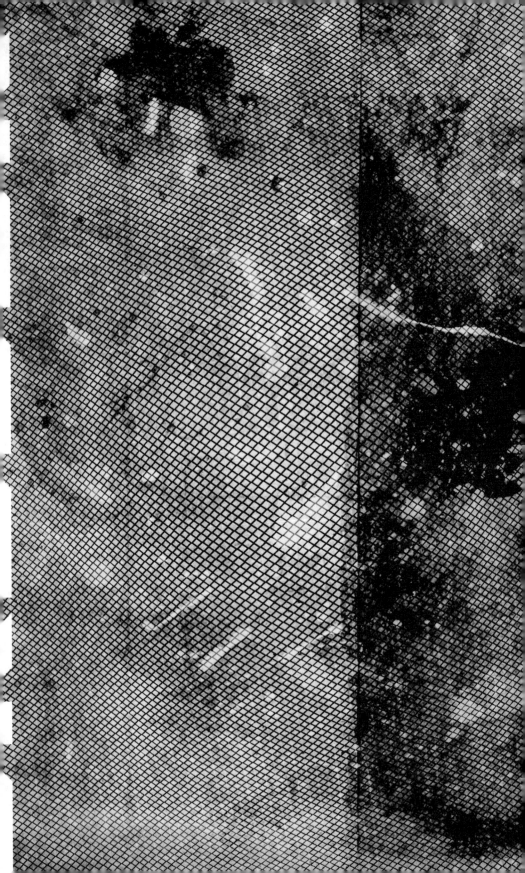

INDEX